WILDLIFE
and PLANTS
of the world

An updated and expanded edition of *Wildlife of the World*

now including plants, microorganisms, and biomes

Volume 17

Classifying organisms	1027	Birds	1046
Simple organisms	1029	Mammals	1048
Nonvascular plants	1030	Glossary	1050
Ferns and their allies	1032	Further Research	1053
Cone-bearing plants	1034	INDEXES	
Flowering plants	1036	Geographic Index	1055
Invertebrates	1038	Biomes Index	1061
Fish	1040	Classification Index	1065
Amphibians	1042	Scientific Names Index	1068
Reptiles	1044	Comprehensive Index	1077

Marshall Cavendish
New York • London • Toronto • Sydney

Marshall Cavendish Corporation
99 White Plains Road
Tarrytown, New York 10591-9001

© Marshall Cavendish Corporation, 1999

Created by **Brown Partworks Ltd**

Library of Congress Cataloging-in-Publication Data

Wildlife and plants of the world.
    p.   cm.
    Includes bibliographical references and index.
    Summary: Alphabetically-arranged illustrated articles introduce over 350 animals, plants, and habitats and efforts to protect them.
    ISBN 0-7614-7099-9 (set : lib. bdg. : alk. paper)
    1. Animals—Juvenile literature. 2. Plants—Juvenile literature.
[1. Animals. 2. Plants.] I. Marshall Cavendish Corporation.
QL49.W539   1998
578—DC21   97-32139
                                CIP
                                AC

ISBN 0-7614-7099-9 (set)
ISBN 0-7614-7128-6 (vol.17)

Printed in Malaysia
Bound in the United States

Brown Packaging

Editorial consultants:
- Joshua Ginsberg, Ph.D.
- Jefferey Kaufmann, Ph.D.
- Paul Sieswerda, Ph.D.
  (Wildlife Conservation Society)
- Special thanks to the Dept. of Botany, The Natural History Museum, U.K.

Editors:	Deborah Evans
	Leon Gray
Assistant editor:	Amanda Harman
Art editors:	Joan Curtis
	Alison Gardner
	Sandra Horth
Picture researchers:	Amanda Baker
	Brenda Clynch
Illustrations:	Bill Botten
	John Francis

Marshall Cavendish Corporation

Editorial director:	Paul Bernabeo
Project editor:	Debra M. Jacobs
Editorial consultant:	Elizabeth Kaplan

PICTURE CREDITS

The publishers would like to thank Natural History Photographic Agency, Ardingly, Sussex, U.K., for supplying the following pictures:
J. Bain 1038; Anthony Bannister 1047; G. I. Bernard 1041, 1049; G. J. Cambridge 1031; Laurie Campbell 1030, 1032, 1034; N. R. Coulton 1033; Stephen Dalton 1036; B. Jones & M. Shimlock 1048; Steve Robinson 1035; Jany Sauvenet 1047.

Additional pictures supplied by:
Corbis 1029; Oxford Scientific Films 1045.

Front cover
Main image: Orangutan female and young, photographed by B. Jones & M. Shimlock.
Additional image: Palm leaf showing vein detail, photographed by G. I. Bernard.

Status

In the Key Facts on the species described in this publication, you will find details of the appearance, name (both Latin and common name wherever possible), breeding habits, and so on. The status of an organism indicates how common it is. The status of each organism is based on reference works prepared by two organizations: *1996 IUCN Red List of Threatened Animals* published by the International Union for Conservation of Nature and Natural Resources (IUCN) and *Endangered and Threatened Wildlife and Plants* published in 1997 by the United States Government Printing Office (USGPO)

Extinct:	No sighting in the last 40 years
Endangered:	In danger of becoming extinct
Threatened:	A species that will become endangered if its present condition in the wild continues to deteriorate
Rare:	Not threatened, but not frequently found in the wild
In captivity:	A species that is extinct in the wild but has been kept successfully in captivity
Feral:	Animals that have been domesticated and have escaped into the wild
Common:	Frequently found within its range, which may be limited
Widespread:	Commonly found in many parts of the world

Classifying organisms

A sense of order is key to understanding the world and any subject. We create that sense of order by naming things. Names are the first things that parents teach their children. On the first day of class, both teachers and students introduce themselves by name. Scientists also name what they study, from astronomy to zoology. Even mathematical formulas can be thought of as names for complex ideas.

The beginnings of classification

In the science of biology, people have been naming living things since the days of the Greek thinker Aristotle (384-322 B.C.E.). He was one of the first to arrange all living things into categories. Scientists who classify living things into groups based on how closely one thing is related to another are called taxonomists. The science of arranging things in groups is called taxonomy, which comes from the Greek word *taxis*, meaning "arrangement."

Understanding which things can be grouped together makes learning easier. You could group animals by where they live, for example, calling all animals that live in the water fish. That would be one way to classify life. However, scientists have decided on a different system. Aristotle was wise enough to see that although dolphins live in the ocean, they are not fish. Because Aristotle noticed that like many land animals, dolphins give birth to live young and nurse their babies with mammary glands, he classified dolphins in the group called mammals.

Almost 2000 years after Aristotle, a Swedish scientist, Carolus Linnaeus (1707-1778), developed a system of naming organisms in which the names themselves identify the particular organism and the group to which it belongs. Each organism

Taxonomic classification of human beings

Type of Classification	Example
Kingdom	Animalia (thirty-two different phyla from dogs to dinosaurs)
Phylum	Chordata (having a hollow nervous system like a spinal chord)
Class	Mammalia (with hair and mammary glands)
Order	Primates (includes monkeys and apes)
Family	*Hominoidea* (having upright posture)
Genus	*Homo* (meaning human)
Species	*sapiens* (meaning wise)

Many children learn this structure by remembering the sentence:
King Phillip Can Order Five Green Snakes

would be called by its species (kind) and its genus (group). The method of assigning two names is similar to the first and last names given to people. Your full name identifies an individual (you) within a group (your family).

Linnaeus named thousands of animals, and his system is the backbone of what we use today. Scientists have agreed on a special form for scientific names. The genus (group) starts with a capital letter and the species (kind) has a small letter. The genus name and the species name are written in italics. For instance, the scientific name for dog is *Canis familiaris* and for the wolf it is *Canis lupus*. You can see that these animals and the names for them are different yet closer than, say, the lion, whose scientific name is *Panthera leo*.

Larger groups

In classification, smaller groups are put into larger groups. Animal species are part of genera (genera is the plural of genus), genera part of families, families part of orders, orders part of classes, classes part of phyla, and phyla part of kingdoms. Plants are divided similarly, except that phyla are referred to as divisions. This system provides a unique name, usually with a Greek or Latin root, that describes the organism (see the box on page 1027). Even if two scientists come from different countries, they can still be sure they are discussing the same organism by using its scientific name.

Keeping up to date

As more is learned and new relationships between living things are discovered, the system of classification must change, too. New species are being found all the time. Recently, new organisms were found deep in the ocean, living in the hot vents of deep-sea fissures (underwater volcanoes). These creatures live without sunlight in a place where no other know organism can survive. Scientists have had to reorganize their classification system to include such strange living things.

Disagreements

Some scientists use three kingdoms, some five, and some would like to use even more. Taxonomists themselves are often classified as lumpers or splitters. Lumpers like a few large categories. Splitters prefer to break up groups into more detailed parts. Throughout the articles in this encyclopedia, the authors have tried to use categories that will be helpful to the reader. There may be other authorities who classify living things differently. Although the rules and standards of classification are established by an International Committee on Nomenclature, debate about the merits of lumping and splitting continues.

For example, some scientists think that the Giant panda is a bear. Others say it is more like a raccoon. The Giant panda's skull and teeth are very like those of the Red panda, which is a member of the raccoon family. Similar characteristics do not always mean animals are closely related. The animals may have evolved similar features because they live in the same habitat or because they eat similar foods. Today most experts agree that the Giant panda is a bear.

Simple organisms

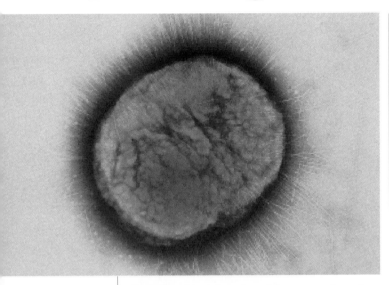

Bacteria, such as Escherichia coli shown above, are part of a large group of organisms called the moneran kingdom. Monerans differ from organisms in other kingdoms because their cells lack a membrane-bound nucleus.

Organisms can be placed into two broad categories based on the structure of their cells. The prokaryotes have cells that contain no defined nucleus. All monerans, from bacteria to blue-green algae, are prokaryotes. In contrast, eukaryotes have cells that have a nucleus surrounded by a cell membrane. All other organisms, from protoctists and fungi to plants and people, are eukaryotes.

The moneran kingdom

Monerans are the simplest and most numerous living organisms. They are found everywhere: in the air, in the soil, and even inside our bodies. Monerans are so small that they can be seen only with a microscope.

All monerans consist of a single, membrane-bound cell protected and supported by a rigid cell wall. Many kinds (species) are rod-shaped or spherical. All monerans are opportunists—they can reproduce very quickly to take advantage

of good conditions. *Escherichia coli* can double their numbers in just 20 minutes. Blue-green algae live mainly in the sea. Giant blooms consisting of billions of them can often be seen from space.

The protoctist kingdom

The protoctist kingdom includes single-celled algae and amoebas. Like monerans, most protoctists are single-celled and visible only under a microscope. However, because their cells contain a membrane-bound nucleus and several tiny membrane-bound organelles, the protoctists are classified as eukaryotes.

Because each organelle performs a different process necessary for the whole cell to stay alive, each process becomes more efficient. Many scientists believe that the organelles were once individual monerans that began to work together. Protoctists share characteristics with animals, plants, and fungi.

The fungi kingdom

The fungi kingdom includes mushrooms, toadstools, and mold. Most fungi consist of many cells, which form long tubes called hyphae. Fungi feed by pushing their hyphae into a host. The host can be living or dead. Many fungi reproduce by releasing tiny spores into the air. The spores are released from the mushrooms and toadstools that push up through the soil. A few kinds of fungi cause disease in humans, but most are beneficial recyclers of organic material.

Nonvascular plants

There are three major groups of nonvascular plants: multicellular algae, mosses, and liverworts. As their name suggests, nonvascular plants lack an inner nutrient-transport (vascular) system. All three groups of nonvascular plants also lack structures that are associated with more complex plants such as the flowering plants (angiosperms). Instead of roots, for example, nonvascular plants have slender, thread-like growths called rhizoids that allow the plant to attach itself to the ground or to other surfaces.

The body cells of nonvascular plants can absorb water and nutrients directly from the environment. Pressure differences inside and outside the plants' cells cause nutrient-rich liquid to move into the cell through the cell membrane. In this way, the cells of nonvascular plants get all the nutrients they need to survive.

Reproduction in nonvascular plants

Nonvascular plants reproduce by a process known as alternation of generations. During one generation (life phase), called the sporophyte phase, the plant produces asexual (neither male nor female) reproductive cells called spores. Spores differ from the seeds of more complex plants, because they do not have to be fertilized to create new plants. When the spores land on a suitable surface, they grow into gametophytes, the second, sexual phase of the plant's life. A gametophyte plant produces male or female sex cells, or both. Male sex cells (sperm) fertilize the

female sex cells (eggs) and new spore-producing (sporophyte) plants develop. The reproductive cycle continues.

The multicellular algae

Brown algae, in the plant division *Phaeophyta,* live primarily in cold ocean waters worldwide. Most of the 1000 different kinds (species) of brown algae are found in the temperate regions along rocky shores or in coastal waters.

The second division, *Rhodophyta,* contains the red algae. Red algae generally prefer warm seawater. Most grow attached to rocks or even to other algae.

Green algae belong to the third plant division, *Chlorophyta.* Most green algae are

KEY FACTS

● **Habitat**
Moist, damp, or wet places; kelp and other seaweeds found in coastal waters

● **Distribution**
Worldwide

● **Characteristics**
Two, often distinct, reproductive life stages; lack vessels for transport of food and water to all cells; lack true leaves, roots, and stems

● **Reproduction**
Alternation of generations: spore-producing (sporophyte) phase and a sexual (gametophyte) phase

● **Evolution**
Many scientists believe that nonvascular plants evolved from a distinct protoctist, unrelated to and separate from the protoctist that gave rise to the vascular plants; others believe that nonvascular plants are a stepping stone in the evolution of the vascular plants

eshwater organisms. Modern land plants might have evolved from the green algae.

Mosses

Most of the 10,000 species of mosses thrive in moist, shady places such as forest floors and bogs around the world. Most mosses are less than 6 in (15 cm) tall and re anchored to soil, bark, or rock by thread-like structures called rhizoids rather than by roots. Mosses have stem-like, rigid tissues that support them. They also have leaf-like lobes, which use sunlight to make food for the plant. The leaf-like lobes of mosses differ from those of more complex plants in that they do not have vascular tissues running through them – the familiar veins in the leaves of flowering plants.

The soft, leafy moss found on rocks and tree trunks is in the gametophyte generation of the moss's life cycle. During this stage, sperm and eggs are produced. Depending on the species, sperm and eggs may be produced on the same or on separate shoots. After fertilization, the united sex cells give rise to the spore-producing (sporophyte) generation of the life cycle. The sporophyte remains attached to the gametophyte and consists of a short stalk on which a spore-producing capsule develops. After dispersal, the spores grow into thread-like structures, which develop into the familiar moss gametophytes. The reproductive cycle continues.

Squishy soils like bogs are often made of Sphagnum mosses. The mosses occur in carpets of shallow, spongy lumps (hummocks), formed by successive layers of growth. Beneath the living, continuously growing surface, layer upon layer of dead moss accumulates. Upper layers compress lower layers until compact peat is formed. People harvest peat, dry it, and use it as heating fuel or to enrich garden soil.

Liverworts

Liverworts get their name from the liver-like lobes that form the gametophyte plant body of some species. Rhizoids anchor liverworts to the moist soil, damp rocks, or tree trunks on which they live. Liverworts are particularly abundant in the tropics, but they also thrive in temperate regions, especially in damp, shady places.

The life cycle of liverworts is similar to that of mosses, showing the same alternation of generations. In addition, (as in many moss species) some species of liverwort can reproduce by means of gemmae. For example, in the liverwort *Marchantia polymorpha,* the gemmae are disk-like structures that develop, grouped together, in tiny gemma cups on the gametophyte. Rain drops may splash gemmae away from the parent plant. Should these gemmae land in suitable areas, they will grow into new gametophytes.

This picture shows the spore-producing (sporophyte) stage of a moss from the group (genus) Polytrichum. *This moss develops ripe, red spore-producing capsules at the tip of short, thread-like stalks. Spores are released from the capsules, disperse, land, and germinate into mosses that bear sex organs – the gametophyte generation.*

Ferns and their allies

Ferns and fern-like plants made the transition from living in water (like algae) or in very wet environments (like moss) to living on land (like rosy maidenhair ferns). As they evolved, land plants developed transporting (vascular) tissues allowing water and nutrients to reach every cell. Some of these plants evolved true leaves, roots, and stems.

Ferns and their relatives (allies) are seedless vascular plants. Though they are more complex than simple, nonvascular plants such as *Sphagnum* mosses and liverworts, they retain a significant characteristic of those simpler plants: they reproduce by spores (reproductive cells that do not have to join with another cell to produce offspring).

Ferns and fern allies undergo two distinct life phases called an alternation of generations. During the more noticeable sporophyte phase, the plant produces asexual reproductive cells called spores. The spores are released and grow into gametophytes, or the sexual phase of the plant's life. Gametophytes produce sperm or eggs. The sperm need moisture to travel to and fertilize the egg. When the eggs are fertilized, they grow into new sporophytes, and the cycle is repeated.

Club mosses, horsetails, whisk ferns, and the true ferns are all spore-producing plants. They make up the fern group.

Club mosses (Subdivision *Lycophyta*)

Club mosses are not mosses at all. They are very ancient vascular plants. The club

◄ *Club mosses live in cool, damp habitats i[n] many parts of the world. This species, F[...] club moss, has made its home at the top o[f] an icy mountain.*

moss you can sometimes see on the moist forest floor is in the sporophyte stage. The spores are produced in spore cases called sporangia that are borne on specialized leaves, called sporophylls. In some different kinds (species) of club moss the sporophylls occur in a cone-like structure at the top of the plant; in others they are in zones along the stems.

Mature, waxy spores are released and land on the ground. If conditions are right, a spore will grow into an underground gametophyte. When the eggs produced by the gametophyte are fertilized, a new, above-ground sporophyte forms.

Today club mosses are often easy to overlook. However, 300-400 million years ago, giant relatives of club mosses dominated the forests. The fossil fuels (coal and gasoline) we use today are the compacted remains of these ancient plants.

KEY FACTS

● **Habitat**
Generally moist, shaded environments such as forest floors; some species have adapted to live in more arid regions

● **Distribution**
Worldwide; particularly in tropics and subtropics

● **Characteristics**
Most have true roots, stems, and leaves; all have vascular tissue for transporting water and nutrients to all cells; seedless

● **Reproduction**
Reproduces by spores; spore-producing phase (sporophyte) is the dominant form

● **Evolution**
Most evolved as land-living plants, though a film of water is needed for fertilization during sexual (gametophyte) life phase

Horsetails (Subdivision *Sphenophyta*)

Horsetails shared ancient forests with club mosses. Today only one group of horsetail exists: the (group) genus *Equisetum*.

The most familiar form of horsetail has delicate green branches, arranged in spirals, which use the sun's energy to make food. At each joint on the stems and branches there is a ring of small leaves.

Spores are formed in cone-like structures. In some species the cones form on the top of the plants. In other species the cones form on a separate, unbranched, brownish-white shoot. Each spore grows into a gametophyte, which may produce either male or female sex organs or both. A new sporophyte emerges from the fertilized egg.

In the days before steel-wool scouring pads horsetails called scouring rushes were used as pot cleaners, because the stem cell walls of the plants contain a rough substance called silica.

Whisk ferns (Subdivision *Psilophyta*)

Despite their name, whisk ferns are not ferns. Only two groups (genera) of this ancient plant group still exist. Species from the group *Psilotum* are vascular plants. These branched, twiggy plants have tiny leaves on their stems. The leaves lack the veins of more complex plants. The stems are flat and green and use the sun's energy to make food. The underground part of the stem has rootlike structures.

The twiggy plant is the whisk fern's spore-producing (sporophyte) form. Spores develop in fused clusters of spore capsules along the branches. If the released spores land on a suitable surface, such as a tree trunk, they grow into tiny gametophytes. Whisk ferns obtain nutrients from their host tree. When the eggs that are produced by the gametophytes are fertilized, they grow into new, sporophytic, whisk ferns.

True ferns (Division *Pterophyta*)

Ferns first appeared on earth about 400 million years ago. However, they are still common, with more than 12,000 living species. Many ferns can be recognized by their graceful, feathery leaves. The leaves, or fronds, are often delicately divided into many sections, which help ferns capture the little sunlight that reaches their forest-floor habitat. Other ferns have simpler, less-divided leaves.

As with most spore-bearing plants, the dominant fern form is the sporophyte. Spores develop on the underside of fronds and form tiny gametophytes when they land on suitable moist surfaces. The gametophytes produce eggs and sperm. The fertilized eggs grow into new ferns.

▼ *Young ferns have attractive, curled-up fronds called fiddleheads, which gradually uncurl to become mature leaves.*

Cone-bearing plants

Cone-bearing plants, or gymnosperms, were the earliest plants to reproduce with seeds. Gymnosperms produce naked seeds that are not enclosed within a fruit (ovary). Instead the seeds lie exposed on the scales of the often-woody cones that bear them. The Greek words *gymnos* and *sperma* together mean "naked seed."

The first gymnosperms were the palm-like cycads and ginkgoes. A few different kinds (species) from these groups still exist. However, the most abundant gymnosperms today are the cone-bearing conifer trees. Conifers dominate many cool temperate and high mountain forests. The last group of gymnosperms, the gnetophytes, are a specialized side branch.

Why seeds?

Seeds are more efficient than reproducing with spores. A fern uses lots of energy producing millions of spores, of which only a few land on sites that are suitable for germination.

A seed is a fertilized egg that is already partially developed. This embryo is surrounded by food stores to nourish it as it develops. The embryo and food stores are encased in a hard, protective covering called the seed coat. The embryo stays safe inside until conditions are right for germination. Unlike flowering plants, gymnosperm seeds are not held in a fruit.

The ginkgo

The oldest gymnosperm fossil is a kind of tree from the group (genus) *Ginkgo*.

▲ *The Scots pine (Pinus sylvestris) is found throughout temperate Europe and northern and western Asia. This tree grows to heights of 70-130 ft (20-40 m). It has a mushroom-shaped crown of foliage on top of a straight trunk measuring 3 ft (1 m) across.*

Around 300 million years ago there were many kinds of ginkgoes. Today there is only one surviving representative of the *Ginkgoaceae* family, *Ginkgo biloba*. This ginkgo tree is native to Asia.

Ginkgo biloba has separate male and female trees (is dioecious). Male trees produce spores called pollen. Wind-borne pollen is carried to the egg-producing structures on female trees. The spore grows into a structure called a male gametophyte. This structure creates a pollen tube that grows toward the egg. When the tube reaches the egg, sperm (male sex cells) is released. Sperm fertilizes the egg, and a seed forms.

Ginkgo biloba is deciduous. In the fall its leaves turn an attractive golden brown and fall to the ground. *Ginkgo biloba* is resistant to air pollution. As a result, this tree is often found in city streets and parks.

The cycads

Cycads are gymnosperms that often resemble palm trees. Today there are 10 groups (genera) of about 100 kinds (species) of cycads, which occur primarily in tropical regions. *Zamia pumila* is the only species native to the United States; it grows in Florida.

Like ginkgoes, cycads are dioecious. The seeds are produced in tiny leaf-like structures clustered together in a cone that forms at the top of the plant. Pollen from cones produced by the male cycad are carried by the wind to the eggs in the cones of female cycads. Once they are fertilized, the eggs develop into seeds in the female cycad's cones.

The conifers

Conifer trees are the most common cone-bearing plants. Conifer forests are found in the colder regions of the earth, closer to the poles than to the equator and high in mountains. Conifers are popularly known as evergreens because they do not lose their leaves in the fall. Conifers generally have needle- or scale-like leaves with a hard, waxy coating.

Conifers such as fir, hemlock, juniper, larch, pine, and spruce produce both male and female cones on the same tree (monoecious). Wind-borne pollen lands on the female cones, where the eggs are fertilized. The fertilized eggs develop into seeds in the female cone. Inside the seed coat, the embryo is surrounded by food reserves. The embryo has seed leaves, or cotyledons. These are tiny, barely-formed leaves, which help the seed to grow after it germinates.

The gnetophytes

There are three groups of gnetophytes: *Ephedra*, *Gnetum*, and *Welwitschia*. The 30 species of *Gnetum* are tropical vine-like plants or trees and have large, leathery leaves. Most *Ephedra* species resemble horsetails and have jointed stems and tiny, scale-like leaves.

Welwitschia mirabilis is the only species from its group. Some botanists have said that this strange plant looks like a giant, stranded octopus. *Welwitschia mirabilis* produces separate, scaly male and female cones. Each scale contains a flower. However, the male flowers also contain nonfertile female flowers. Once the eggs of a female cone are fertilized, the flowers of *Welwitschia mirabilis* produce seeds that are enclosed in a structure resembling a fruit or nut – just like flowering plants.

Gnetophytes also have vessels in their woody tissue. Vessels are stacks of cells that extend through the wood and provide pathways for water moving through the plant. A similar transport system occurs in the flowering plants (angiosperms).

▲ **Welwitschia mirabilis** *is an unusual plant that grows in the deserts of southwestern Africa.*

KEY FACTS

● **Habitat**

Ginkgoes: temperate climate; cycads: tropical and subtropical regions; gnetophytes: tropical regions (*Gnetum*) and deserts (*Ephedra* and *Welwitschia*); conifers: cold temperate forests and high altitudes

● **Distribution**

Worldwide

● **Characteristics**

Produces naked seeds in cones

● **Reproduction**

Sperm and eggs usually produced in cones on separate plants; pollen carried by wind to female cones; fertilized egg develops into bare seed in female cone; bare seed contains embryo with seed leaves surrounded by food stores

● **Evolution**

Development of seed surrounded by food stores and encased in a protective seed coat enabled the seed to germinate even after waiting for suitable growing conditions. The gnetophytes' reproductive features indicate that they may be distantly related to flowering plants

Flowering plants

Flowering plants, or angiosperms, are the most successful land plants on earth. There are over 235,000 different kinds (species) of flowering plants, comprising over 90 percent of all known plants.

Angiosperms

The word "angiosperm" comes from the Greek word *angion,* meaning "vessel." The seeds of these plants are enclosed in a seed case or ovary (the vessel) which eventually becomes the fruit.

There are two major groups of flowering plants. Each group is defined by the kind of seed leaf (called a cotyledon)

▲ *The honeybee is the insect most commonly involved in cross-pollinating flowers such as the apple blossom above. As the bee travels from flower to flower, grains of pollen cling to its body and are often deposited within another flower, thus pollinating the plant.*

the plants' seeds have. During its development inside the seed coat, the inner seed grows either one or two seed leaves. Plants that grow one seed leaf are called monocotyledons (monocots for short). Plants that grow two seed leaves are called dicotyledons, or dicots. Cotyledons store food to help the sprouting seed grow. They are also able to use the sun's energy to make food.

The dicots were the first flowering plants to evolve. Today there are about 170,000 species of dicots. Many are herbs, shrubs, and trees. There are about 65,000 species of monocots. Lilies, orchids, palms, and grasses are all monocots.

The key to success

The main reason for the success and diversity of angiosperms is the development of the flower. Male sex cells (called pollen) develop in the flower's stamen. Each stamen has a swollen portion at its tip called the anther. Pollen grains form in the anther.

Female sex cells (eggs) grow inside ovaries in the flower's thread-like filament, the pistil. At the tip of the pistil is a tiny, sticky structure called the stigma. A hollow tube, called the style, runs the length of the pistil's center and ends in a round ovary. The ovary contains one or more ovules.

The sticky stigma catches the tiny pollen grains, which pass through the style and fertilize (join with) the flower's female egg cells in the ovules. After fertilization, the

vules develop into embryonic plants ontained within seeds.

How pollen reaches the ovule

ollination is the method by which ollen reaches and joins with the female ex cells. Most flowers contain both nale and female reproductive structures. elf-pollination can occur if pollen from ne male part of the flower joins with ne female part of the same flower or nother flower of the same plant.

When pollen from one plant reaches the istil of a flower from another plant, this is ermed cross-pollination. Cross-pollination epends on the pollen being transported rom plant to plant. Insects such as ants, ees, butterflies, and beetles are the most miliar pollen carriers. Birds and small nammals may also transport pollen grains.

Many flowers are wind-pollinated. ollen from one plant's flower is ransported to the stigma of another plant y air currents. Wind-pollinated plants roduce vast quantities of pollen grains.

Scientists estimate that some flowers may produce over one million pollen grains for each egg available for fertilization.

Seeds and their dispersal

To develop into new plants, seeds must be carried to a place where they can grow. Fruits are seed-containing structures. Many fruits are brightly colored and have a sweet taste to attract animals. The animals swallow the seeds whole, and the hard seed coat protects the seed as it passes through the animal's digestive system. The undigested seed then emerges with the animal's waste products. Seeds may also be transported externally. Squirrels are famous for hoarding acorns in underground larders. However, the squirrel may forget where it has buried the acorns. Those seeds may develop into new trees when conditions become right for germination to occur.

▼ *The main parts of a flower. The petals are often brightly colored to attract insects.*

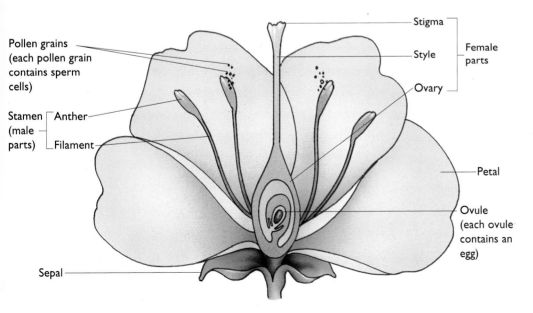

Pollen grains (each pollen grain contains sperm cells)

Stamen (male parts) — Anther — Filament

Sepal

Stigma
Style — Female parts
Ovary

Petal

Ovule (each ovule contains an egg)

Invertebrates

Invertebrates are the most numerous animals on earth. So far, nearly 1.2 million species have been identified. This accounts for nearly 97 percent of all known animal species.

Patterns of development

Since there are so many different types of invertebrates, there are few features common to all species. They are all animals without a backbone, made up of a large number of individual cells. However, the systems that keep them alive (their nervous, sensory, digestive, circulatory, and reproductive systems) vary widely.

Invertebrates existed on earth over 700 million years ago. No one knows exactly how they evolved, but it was probably from a type of primitive single-celled animal called a protozoan.

Of the 30 or so phyla (scientific divisions) of invertebrates, the simplest are probably the *Porifera*, or sponges. Sponges have very few features usually associated with animals. Their skin is only one cell layer thick, while most animals' skins have two or three cell layers. Their bodies are supported by a framework of minute rigid structures (spicules), while other animals have external or internal skeletons. Sponges have no organized nervous system. They also have no central circulatory or digestive system so each cell must take in its own nutrition.

The most complex invertebrates are the mollusks. Cephalopods such as squids,

▲ *Octopuses are the most intelligent of all invertebrates. They also have the most complex nervous system found in this group.*

ctopuses, and cuttlefish have three layers o their skin, an internal skeleton of artilage (which is slightly flexible), and istinct body parts. Their large and omplex brains give them fast reactions, naking them agile hunters. Their sensory rgans are also well developed.

Reproduction

All invertebrates can reproduce, ometimes by sexual reproduction (mating vith the opposite gender), sometimes by sexual reproduction (without a mate), nd some invertebrates can reproduce oth ways. One form of asexual eproduction is found in those nvertebrates that are able to grow new ndividuals from severed parts of their odies, such as a bit of tail. Most sponges, ydras, jellyfish, flatworms, and starfish, s well as many other invertebrates, can eproduce in this way.

Metamorphosis

Many invertebrates produce offspring that re completely unlike the adult. These are enerally called larvae. In most species this s the primary feeding stage. Larvae allow nvertebrates to inhabit two different nvironments, making the best use of oth. As larvae grow they undergo netamorphosis. With each stage they look nore and more like the adult. Insects learly display this type of development.

Locomotion

nvertebrates have many different methods f getting about. In some simple animals uch as sponges and corals, the animals an only move during the brief larval stage

of life. Some of the invertebrates that live in water use hairs (cilia) or tails (flagella) to get around.

Many mollusks glide through the water by wriggling their bodies. Land-based slugs and snails have to secrete a layer of slime to lubricate the surface on which they move. The more advanced mollusks such as squids and octopuses use jet propulsion to push themselves through the water. They draw water into their bodies and then force it out powerfully.

Arthropods (creatures with jointed limbs) have evolved more specialized ways to move. Early crustaceans, such as the cave-dwelling *Speleonectes*, have long segmented bodies similar to their worm-like ancestors. Each body segment bears a pair of simple legs. These crustaceans swim through the water by moving their legs in a wave along their bodies, like a series of oars.

As land invertebrates developed, the segments of their bodies became more specialized and fused together. All insects have three pairs of legs that are attached to the central group of segments, the part of the body called the thorax.

The power of flight

Insects are the only invertebrates that have developed wings. Four growths from the top of the thorax eventually became wings. Most insects have two pairs of wings during their adult stage. Many species (including all the beetles) use the forewings, or elytra, as covers for the more delicate hind wings. In the fastest and most agile fliers, the hindwings are smaller and act as stabilizers.

KEY FACTS

- **Largest at sea**
  The largest invertebrate is the Giant Atlantic squid; these mollusks can reach lengths of over 60 ft (18 m) long and can weigh in excess of 2200 lb (1,000 kg)

- **Largest on land**
  The largest land invertebrate is the robber crab; these giant relatives of the hermit crab can reach leg spans of over 3 ft (1 m)

- **Fast breeder**
  One of the fastest reproducing insects is the aphid; each female can produce 5 offspring a day after only 10 days of life, producing around 100 baby aphids in her life time; if allowed to breed unchecked for 8 months, a single aphid would produce a final population of 1,000,000,000,000 (10^{12})

- **Large incubator**
  The adult pork tapeworm can have as many as 1600 segments; each segment may contain over 70,000 embryos, so each female can incubate up to 112,000,000 babies at one time

Fish

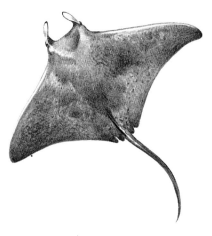

Fish are vertebrates, or animals with backbones. Like reptiles and amphibians, fish are cold blooded, which means that their body temperature varies with the temperature of the water. All fish need oxygen to survive; they have structures called gills that take oxygen from the water.

Fish have fins that propel or help to propel them through the water. More than 20,000 species of fish live in the

▲ *The ray (top left) and the lamprey (above) are typical of the two smaller classes of fish, cartilaginous fish (which do not have bony skeletons) and jawless fish. Most fish, including salmon, are bony fish (below).*

world's waters. Together they comprise three classes: fish with skeletons of cartilage (rays and sharks), jawless fish (lampreys and hagfish), and bony fish, the largest class.

Elastic skeletons

There are 700 species of cartilaginous fish. Cartilage is a tough, elastic material, which is found in the nose and ears of the human body. Lampreys and hagfish also have a cartilaginous skeleton, but they are in a separate group because they do not have jaws.

The bony fish have jaws and a bony skeleton. Although they vary widely in shape and size, nearly all of them are recognizable as typical fish.

The typical fish

A typical fish usually has seven fins, including the tail fin. Each fin plays a part

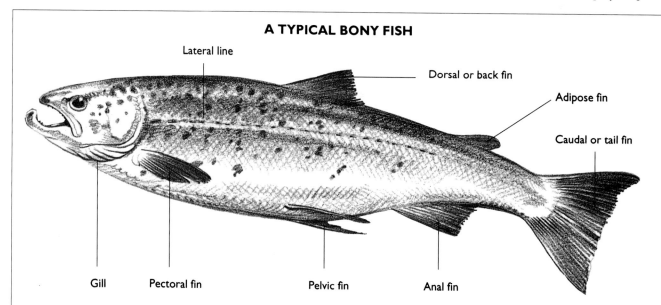

A TYPICAL BONY FISH

Lateral line

Dorsal or back fin

Adipose fin

Caudal or tail fin

Gill

Pectoral fin

Pelvic fin

Anal fin

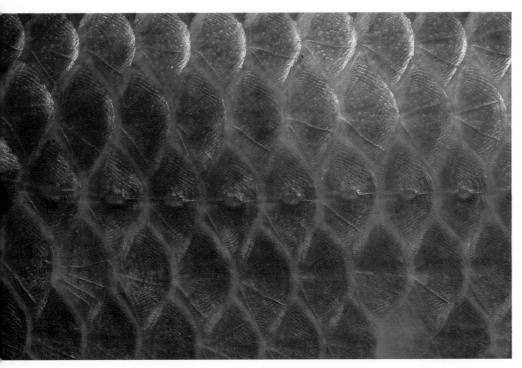

◄ *Many of the bony fish are covered in tiny overlapping scales. In this picture of a carp you can see the lateral line. The line is a row of pores that opens into a canal containing tiny organs that carry messages to the brain.*

in swimming and balancing. The fins are really folds of skin that are stretched over a framework of fine but hard spines. Embedded in the skin on both sides of the body is a sensory organ called the lateral line. This organ enables the fish to detect objects that are around it.

Breathing

A fish breathes by taking in oxygen from water. The water flows in through the mouth and passes over the gills, which are located just behind the eye. Gills are thin folds of skin that contain thousands of tiny blood vessels. Oxygen passes into the bloodstream via blood vessels.

Getting through the water

Fish swim in different ways. Some move like snakes; others wag their tail fins so that they move like paddles while keeping the rest of the body still. Still other fish uses the last third of the body for

propulsion, alternately contracting the strong muscles on either side of its tail.

Most bony fish have an organ called a swim bladder, or air sac, which is filled with gases. The swim bladder keeps the fish afloat in the water so that it does not have to move its tail and fins constantly to remain buoyant.

Breeding

In fish, the breeding process is known as spawning. At the beginning of the breeding season the reproductive organs of the male and female swell, and the sperm and eggs begin to ripen. Most fish then travel to breeding grounds, where the eggs and sperm are released into the water so that fertilization can take place. In some cases, the breeding ground is within the usual habitat in a place where the developing eggs will be undisturbed. However, some fish, such as eels and salmon, travel hundreds of miles to breed.

KEY FACTS

● **Breathing**
Lungfish and mudskippers can take in oxygen from the air; lungfish, as their name suggests, have lungs as humans and other mammals do, but mudskippers are also thought to be able to take in oxygen from the air through their skin

● **Scales**
Sticklebacks have bony plates (scutes) on their bodies instead of scales

● **Lights**
The skin of some fish has special organs that give off light; these fish live in the ocean depths, where very little light, if any, filters down from the surface of the sea; one example is the group of deep-sea angler fish

Amphibians

Frogs and toads, newts and salamanders, and a group of little-known, wormlike creatures called caecilians are all grouped together as amphibians. Altogether there are about 100 species of caecilians, 360 species of salamanders, and 3000 species of frogs and toads, making a total of about 3500. New species are being discovered in some of the more remote parts of the world, but several species have become extinct quite recently and many are dying out, largely as a result of habitat destruction and pollution.

A double life

Because amphibians have backbones they are classed as vertebrates, along with the fish, reptiles, birds, and mammals. The earliest amphibians appeared 350 million years ago when they developed from fish that left the water and began to live on the land.

These early amphibians could probably not stray far from the water's edge because they were not completely adapted to living on the land. Over countless generations, they evolved more efficient lungs and limbs and so were able to spread to a whole new range of habitats.

Amphibians are still closely associated with water, however, and in a way they

▼ After mating, the female frog lays eggs. The tadpoles eat their way out of the jelly-like capsules that surround the eggs. The tadpoles swim freely through the water, gradually growing and changing shape.

▲ After a period of development that can last from a few weeks to several months, the tadpoles begin to develop limbs and lungs. Finally, they are able to leave the water and breathe air.

are animals that live two separate lives: one in the water, as young, or larvae, and one on the land, as adults. The word "amphibian" comes from two Greek words that mean "double-life."

Breeding in water

Amphibian eggs have no shells and would dry out if they were laid on the land, so the animals have to return to ponds, swamps, streams, or rivers to breed. In North America and Europe, this usually takes place during the spring. The females lay eggs in clumps, in strings, or singly, and may attach them to underwater plants or stones. Most species hatch from eggs and become tadpoles (larvae). The tadpoles begin to feed and grow in their watery environment. If they are to become frogs or toads, their tails will be absorbed into their bodies and then they will have completed the change from gill-breathing larvae to air-breathing adults. The same events occur in newt and salamander larvae, except, of course, that they keep their tails. At this stage most species leave the water to begin the next phase of their lives as adults.

There are a few specialized amphibians that miss out on the water stage altogether, and there are also a few in

which the adults never leave their watery environment, although the vast majority follow the typical pattern.

Breathing through skin

Amphibians also rely on damp and humid places to breathe properly. Although most species have lungs, these are often not very efficient. The animals make up for this by breathing through their skin as well. Some species use their skin almost entirely for breathing. The salamanders in one family, for instance, have no lungs at all and rely totally on their skin as a surface for respiration. The skin's surface must be moist to allow gases to be exchanged. Special glands under the skin's surface continually secrete fluid, which is why amphibians have a cold, wet, and rather slimy feel.

If an amphibian's skin becomes too dry, it cannot breathe properly and it will die. Some species are better adapted to dry conditions than others, however, and there are a few frogs and toads that live in deserts. The Spadefoot toad, for instance, burrows down into the sand during the summer and forms a cocoon of shed skin around its body. This cocoon prevents the toad from drying out completely and the animal stays in this state until heavy rains come. Then the toad tunnels rapidly up to the surface and breeds in temporary ponds and flooded fields. Its tadpoles must develop and metamorphose quickly before the water evaporates.

Amphibians of the rainforest

Most species of amphibians live in damp places, especially in tropical rainforests,

▲ *Scientists have named 163 species of caecilians, worm-like creatures found in tropical regions. They are related to salamanders and frogs.*

where the number of species as well as the number of individuals are greater than in any other habitat. In the tropics, amphibians can be found in a huge variety of shapes, sizes, and colors: they can find lots of small insects to eat, and they have plenty of moist habitats in which to live.

Because there are so many amphibians in the same area, they have evolved in many different ways to coexist. There are salamanders and frogs that live in the tree tops and never come down to the ground; they even lay their eggs in the small puddles of water that collect between the leaves of air plants.

Other species live in leaf litter; some of these are so leaf-like in appearance that they are almost invisible, especially in the dim and gloomy conditions on the forest floor. Some frogs, notably the arrow poison frogs from the Amazon rainforest, have highly poisonous substances in their skin. These species are not camouflaged at all, but are brilliantly colored so that predators recognize and avoid eating them.

Reptiles

Reptiles form one of the most important classes of animals, dating back to the "Age of Reptiles," 280 to 65 million years ago, when dinosaurs and other prehistoric reptiles ruled the earth. Scientists know of about 6500 living species, which are divided into several groups, or orders: the turtles, terrapins, and tortoises; the crocodilians (crocodiles and their relatives); and the lizards, worm lizards, and snakes.

The oldest group reptiles are the turtles and the crocodilians. Turtles are found in the warmer parts of the world, including the tropical oceans where the largest turtles live, and the deserts. The alligators and crocodiles, of which there are 25

▼ *Reptiles have different shaped tongues. Some lizards have flat tongues that they flick in and out of their mouths (A). Other lizards and most snakes have forked tongues (B) that they constantly flick in and out of their mouths, picking up scent molecules from the air. The chameleons have a special use for their tongues. They can extend them to a length equivalent to their own body length — up to 16 in (40 cm) in some cases (C). The tongue has a sticky tip to trap the insects that the chameleon eats.*

species, and the tuatara (a strange lizard-like reptile from New Zealand) have also survived from prehistoric times. These groups of reptiles survived for so long because they were either well adapted to their habitat or have since been able to adapt to changing conditions.

Successful animals

Reptiles differ from amphibians in having a scaly skin (even turtles, which have a bony shell and scales on their limbs, tail neck, and head). The scales stop them from losing too much water through their skin when the weather is hot and dry. Perhaps even more important, the early reptiles developed an egg with a tough shell that protected the contents. This meant that they could lay their eggs on land. In contrast, amphibians have soft eggs that need water for protection.

Scaly skins and shelled eggs were the keys to the reptiles' success. These features allowed them to colonize areas where there was little water and let them exploit unoccupied habitats. Although some reptiles (for example, crocodiles and turtles) are found near water, many are found in deserts where few other animals could survive.

Cold blooded

Reptiles evolved before the birds and the mammals and they differ from these groups in one very important way. Birds and mammals make their own heat inside their bodies and keep their

A

B

C

KEY FACTS

- **Snake**
Two of the largest snakes are the Reticulated python from Southeast Asia and the anaconda from South America; each is almost 33 ft (10 m) long

- **Crocodile**
The largest crocodilians are the saltwater crocodiles, which may grow up to 30 ft (9 m) long, but more often are 16-20 ft (5-6 m); a crocodile 20 ft (6 m) long would weigh up to 2300 lb (1040 kg)

- **Lizard**
The Komodo dragon is the world's largest lizard and may measure up to 10 ft (3 m) in length

- **Turtle**
The largest turtle is the leatherback; it can grow to 6 ft (1.8 m) and weigh 1300 lb (590 kg)

- **Tortoise**
The giant tortoises from the Galápagos Islands measure up to 4 ft (1.2 m) long

- **Small lizards**
The smallest reptiles are lizards; some geckos from South America are fully grown at 2 in (5 cm)

▲ *Lizards that rest on the bark of trees may be gray in color but they may also have markings that resemble lichens and mosses growing there.*

...ody temperature constant. Reptiles have ...o rely on the temperature of the air ...round them to cool or warm their ...odies. In cold climates, this can be a ...isadvantage because the animals can only ...e active when the weather is warm. ...ome reptiles have adapted to these ...onditions by basking in the sun during ...he day and hibernating at night. ...lowever, in general there are fewer ...eptiles in the cooler parts of the world ...han in the tropics.

Different lifestyles

...eptiles have evolved many different ...festyles. Some species, such as many ...zards and tortoises, are strict vegetarians ...hat eat leaves and flowers. Others, ...owever, especially the crocodilians and ...he snakes, are efficient hunters, preying ...pon many other animals. Some have specialized diets. The African egg-eating snake, for example, eats only birds' eggs, and several snakes from South America and Asia eat only slugs and snails. Most reptiles, however, eat a variety of foods.

The way each species hunts for its food depends on a number of factors. Some just sit and wait for their prey to come wandering past. Then they strike quickly and effectively. Chameleons and rattlesnakes are good examples of "sit and wait" hunters.

Other reptiles actively search for their food. These include the vegetarian species such as desert tortoises, which may have to cover a large area to find enough food to keep them alive and healthy.

Birds

A

B

C

There are over 9500 species of birds alive today. These make up a clearly defined group of animals with many of the same physical features. Even the more unusual birds, such as penguins or kiwis, have things in common with all other birds.

All birds have feathers, a beak, two eyes, a pair of wings, and two legs. Penguins' feathers are fine and tightly packed to give them a sleek, waterproof coat. Their wings act like flippers. Flightless birds have downy feathers. For most birds, feathers and wings are essential to their survival, giving them the ability to fly.

Feathers and flight

There are different types of feathers. Each feather has a central shaft and feathery barbs, which may be stiff or soft.

Soft downy feathers are usually close to the skin. They provide insulation but cannot be used for flight.

Body feathers are the small feathers covering the entire body, including all the downy parts. They streamline the body when the birds are in flight or swimming under water.

In most birds the flight feathers are the most colorful. They are long and strong, and shaped so that one side forms the leading edge when the bird flies.

◀ *Downy feathers (A) are close to the skin; they do not have strong barbs, so they cannot be used for flight. Small feathers (B) cover the body giving a sleek shape. Flight feathers (C) are long and strong with the central shaft set to one side.*

Molting

Most birds lose all their feathers and grow new ones at least once a year. In most species this is a fairly continuous process, in which the feathers fall out and are replaced in stages so that the bird does not lose its ability to fly. In other species, especially ducks, geese, and swans, all the flight feathers are lost at the same time so that for a few weeks the birds cannot fly.

Other things in common

All birds have toes and claws. Most have four toes: three pointing forward and one pointing backward. All birds also have bills or beaks (the two words are used interchangeably). The beak has two parts, which are fixed to the skull and lower jaw, so that they serve the same purpose as the teeth of mammals.

Eggs and nests

All birds lay eggs. Nearly all species care for their eggs and young to ensure that as many as possible survive. Part of the caring process usually involves nest building. Nests may be no more than a hollow scraped in the ground or sticks piled in a treetop. The nests are usually lined with soft grass, moss, or mud so that the eggs will be protected and the young will have a comfortable home.

Parental care

Some chicks are well developed when they hatch. Ground-dwelling birds, including the flightless birds, game birds,

nd water fowl, are able to follow their
arents almost as soon as they hatch. The
erching birds tend to be poorly
eveloped but grow very rapidly on a
liet of insects and seeds.

Young birds of prey and many sea birds
ake a long time to develop. The parents
ontinue to feed them for many months
ntil they have developed true flight
eathers rather than the down that covered
hem when they hatched. When the young
eave the nest they can fly well and soon
earn to hunt for themselves.

A few species of birds have communal
rrangements for the care of the young.
lamingoes, for example, lay their eggs
n mounds of mud in the shallow lakes
f Africa or in river deltas. Once the eggs
atch, the young birds cluster together in
roups. There are always some adults with
he young, but all the parents fly off to
eeding grounds at some time and return
o feed their own chicks with a special
nilk that they make in their crops (part
f their necks).

Some birds do not care for their young,
uch as the megapodes, or incubator birds.
Megapodes live in Southeast Asia and
Australia. They lay their eggs in mounds
f rotting vegetation that they build on the
orest floor or in loose sand or volcanic
lust. After laying, the birds leave their
ggs to incubate in the warmth of the
nest. When the young hatch, they burrow
heir way out and run off to forage for
hemselves. The young are able to fly
vithin hours of hatching.

A few birds leave the work of rearing
heir young to other, unrelated birds.
The European cuckoo, for example, lays
its eggs in the nests of other birds. The
owner of the nest (the host) incubates
the eggs and feeds and rears the young.
Often, the young cuckoo throws other
eggs or nestlings out of the nest to make
room for itself.

A helping hand

You can help garden birds find a safe
nesting site by providing a birdhouse with
a hole in the side. Small birds such as
bluebirds prefer small holes, less than 1¼
in (3 cm) in diameter. Larger birds such
as blackbirds and cardinals are happy with
a wide opening across the top of the front
of the birdhouse. Birdhouses should be at
least 6 ft (2 m) from the ground, out of
direct sunlight, and out of the reach of
cats and squirrels.

▲ Ostriches simply lay their eggs in a shallow
hollow. The male watches over them.

Mammals

◀ *Orangutans are quiet by nature. They like to live in a small group, usually made up of an adult female and her offspring.*

One of the most important distinguishing features common to all mammals is that their young feed on their mother's milk. Mammals also have a covering of hair or fur on their bodies. Although there are some exceptions, all mammals have these features at some stage in their lives.

Most mammals have four limbs, usually with five toes on each foot. Sea mammals' limbs are flippers, while whales have lost their hind limbs altogether. Mammals are warm-blooded animals. While the temperature of cold-blooded animals rises and falls with the temperature of their surroundings, a mammal's body stays more or less at the same temperature. Since they are warm blooded, mammals can be active at any time, day or night.

Mammals as social animals

It is a characteristic of many mammals that they are social animals, and for those that live in groups social life is very important.

Although some mammals are solitary, among them the fox, bobcat, and orangutan, most benefit in one way or another from living with other members of the species.

A group of mammals may be only a small family unit consisting of a mother and her young, as in the bears, or it may consist of thousands of animals living in herds on the open plains, as in the mixed herds of zebra and antelopes on the great savannahs of Africa. In the family unit, the young are not only protected by their elders but also learn to become adults. Some other groups of mammals have developed mutually beneficial relationships; for example, the chitals (Indian deer) are often found with groups of monkeys: the monkeys eat the stalks of a particular plant, dropping the leaves to the deer waiting below. The monkeys benefit because the deer have sharper hearing and sense danger before the monkeys do.

The amount of time young mammals spend in the family depends on a number of factors, including how developed they

re at birth, how long they live, and how he group is organized. For example, oofed mammals that are born in open ountry where there is little natural rotection have to be able to run swiftly hen predators such as lions give chase. Many are able to stand almost immediately fter they are born and walk and run soon fter that. Such mammals usually reach dulthood very quickly; Burchell's zebra ecome sexually mature after 16-22 nonths, although they may not breed until hey are two years old. Other mammals, owever, do not need to be so developed t birth, especially if they are born in laces that are well hidden from predators. These mammals may even be born blind nd naked. They need the protection of heir mothers for much longer.

The benefits of living in groups are more han giving protection for the young and iving them the opportunity to learn from he adults. There is safety in numbers. In a erd of caribou or a colony of prairie dogs here are many pairs of eyes, ears, and ostrils for picking up signs of danger, so hat the other members can be forewarned nd run for cover.

The Musk ox have a particular way of roviding protection for cows and calves vhen the group is threatened. Facing utward so that they can attack the redator with their horns, the massive ulls form a circle with the cows and alves well protected in the center.

Mammal defenses

Mammals have other ways of defending hemselves beside living in groups. Some ave sharp spines that cover almost every part of the body (the porcupine, echidna, and hedgehog), others have bony plates (the armadillo and pangolin), and still others give off strong, foul-smelling scents (the skunk), or have nasty-tasting flesh (the shrews). In many species, the color of the mammals' coat helps them to blend in with their surroundings and thus escape detection. Mammals that live in deserts are usually a light brown or other pale color, like the surrounding sands. Some mammals that live in the Arctic and other areas with cold, snowy winters have white coats in the winter. The vivid black and white stripes of the zebra break up the outline of the zebra's body, making it difficult for predators to aim their attack, but zebras also have other lines of defense. They are built for speed and can often outrun their pursuers, and, when cornered, can be very aggressive, lashing out with their hoofs and biting with their teeth. Some mammals, however, have few natural predators and rely on their sheer size as a defense. These are large beasts such as the elephant and rhinoceros.

▼ *The jaguar is a solitary animal. It has so many defensive skills that it does not need to live in a group for protection. A savage fighter, its sharp claws are deadly. It can run quickly, is an excellent swimmer, and is able to climb trees. The largest cat to be found in South America, its beautiful coat provides it with camouflage.*

Glossary

Abdomen

The part of the body that contains most of the digestive tract (as in vertebrates); the rear part of the body, usually forming its bulk (as in insects and spiders)

Alpine meadow

An area at high elevation, above the tree line, where plants grow

Angiosperm

Plant that has flowers and whose seeds are enclosed in fruits

Annual plant

Plant that completes its life cycle in one growing season

Anther

Pollen-bearing portion of the stamen

Aquatic

Living in water

Asexual

An organism that lacks functional sex organs

Berry

A pulpy fruit, usually edible, varying in structure, but always small in size

Biennial plant

Plant that takes two growing seasons to complete its life cycle

Bud

A young shoot, usually protected by leaves

Bulb

A short, flattened, or disk-shaped underground stem, with many fleshy leaves filled with stored food

Canopy

The uppermost layer of a forest

Carnivore

Any meat-eating animal

Carnivorous plant

Plant that can digest animals

Carrion

The decaying flesh of a dead animal

Cellulose

Complex sugar that is the main constituent of plant cell walls

Clone

Group of genetically identical organisms produced by asexual reproduction

Compound leaf

A leaf whose blade is divided into several distinct leaflets

Corm

A short, solid, vertical, enlarged stem that stores food

Cross-pollination

The transfer of pollen from a stamen of the flower on one plant to the stigma of a flower on another plant

Culm

The stem of a monocotyledon (such as a grass)

Deciduous

Trees and shrubby plants that lose their

leaves in the fall and grow new ones in spring

Defoliate

To strip trees and bushes of their leaves

Deforestation

The process of removing trees from an area

Dicotyledon

A flowering plant that has an embryo with two seed leaves

Dioecious plant

Having the male and female parts in different individuals

Display

A pattern of activity where a creature shows off to others

Diurnal

Active during the day

Ecology

The relationship between a living organism and its environment

Embryo

An early stage of animal or plant development; the organism is still inside its mother, an egg, or a seed

Epiphyte

A plant that uses another plant for support while it grow

Evergreen

Trees and shrubs that keep their leaves through more than on growing season

Fertilization

When a male sperm penetrates a female eg to create offspring

Filament

Stalk of the stamen

Fledgling

A young bird that has grown its feathers

Florets

Small flowers that make up the composit flower or the spike of the grasses

Fruit
The mature ovary of flowering plants that encloses the seeds

Germination
The beginning of growth of a seed, spore, bud, or other structure

Gestation
The process of growth of an embryo inside a mammal's body; pregnancy

Gymnosperm
A plant whose seeds are not enclosed in an ovary; seeds are often held in cones instead

Habitat
The environment in which a species is normally found

Herb
A seed plant that does not develop woody tissues

Herbivore
Any plant-eating animal

Hibernate
To spend the winter in an inactive or dormant state

Home range
The area normally traveled by an individual during its life span

Host
A plant or animal in or on which another plant or animal lives

Incubation
The time an embryo in an egg takes to develop before hatching

Inflorescence
A cluster of flowers on top of a stem

Insectivore
Any insect-eating animal

Invertebrate
Any animal that does not have a backbone

Larva
The young stage of an invertebrate

Liana
A plant that climbs on other plants for support; a plant with climbing shoots

Marine
Living in the sea

Metamorphosis
A change of form during an animal's life cycle, from egg, through larva and pupa, to adult

Migration
The process of moving from one area to another, usually with the change of season

Monocotyledon
A flowering plant that has an embryo with one seed leaf

Monoecious plant
Having separate male and female parts on the same individual

Nestling
A young bird that has not yet learned to fly

Nocturnal
Active at night

Nurse
To provide milk (from the mother's teats) for a baby mammal

Omnivore
A creature that eats both plants and animals

Ovary
In plants, the enlarged portion at the base of the pistil, which becomes the fruit

Parasite
A plant or animal that depends on a host but does not give benefit to the host

Perennial plant
A plant that grows year after year

Permafrost
A permanently frozen layer at variable depth below the surface in cold regions of a planet (as in earth's tundra)

Photosynthesis
A process by which light energy is converted to the chemical energy stored in chemical compounds; it occurs in plants, blue-green algae, and some other types of bacteria

Pistil
Central organ of the flower, typically consisting of the ovary, style, and stigma

Pollen
A mass of male sex cells in a seed plant that looks like fine dust

Pollination
The transfer of pollen from the male to the female part of a flower

Predator
Any species that hunts other species

Prehensile
Fingers, toes, or a tail that can grip

Prey
An animal that is hunted by another animal

Pupa
The stage in an insect's life cycle between larva and adult

Range
The parts of the world in which a particular species is found

Rhizome
An underground stem that stores food and produces new plants

Roosting
Sleeping birds

Rosette

A cluster of fully expanded leaves growing in crowded circles or spirals

Seed

The matured female sex cell; that is, after pollination by the male sex cell

Seed leaf

A flowering plant's first leaf, which develops inside the seed

Seed plant

A plant that produces seeds

Self-pollination

The transfer of pollen from the stamen to the stigma of either the same flower or flowers on the same plant

Sepal

Outermost flower parts; they enclose the other parts in the bud

Shoot

A young branch that shoots out from the main trunk of a tree, or the young main portion of a plant growing above ground

Spawn

To produce eggs in large quantities; used to describe the way fish, mollusks, coral, and amphibians lay eggs (often unfertilized) under water

Spike

A type of elongated inflorescence commonly found in grasses in which the flowers are attached directly by their base

Sporangium

A spore case

Spore

The reproductive unit produced by plants, fungi, protoctists, and bacteria. Spores develop into a plant without joining with another cell

Stamen

Flower structure made up of the male reproductive organ attached to a stalk or filament

Stigma

Part of the style in plants to which pollen adheres

Stoma

Small pore in the surface of plants through which gases pass

Strobilus

One of the modified leaves or scales grouped together on the stem of club mosses and horsetails; the cone of a gymnosperm

Style

Slender column of tissue that arises from the top of the ovary and through which the pollen tube grows

Symbiosis

A relationship between organisms that benefit from living close to one another

Subarctic

Regions immediately outside of the Arctic Circle

Subtropical

Regions bordering the tropical zone

Tableland

A broad, level, elevated area

Taproot

A plant's main root

Temperate

Regions between the Tropic of Cancer and the Arctic Circle or between the Tropic of Capricorn and the Antarctic Circle; climate is usually moderate, and the growing season is around six months

Tendril

A special kind of leaf or stem found on climbing plants; the tendril wraps around other objects and supports the growing plant

Terrestrial

Living on land

Territory

The area occupied by a single animal or group of animals, to the exclusion of others of the same species; often defended by aggressive displays

Transpiration

The evaporation of water from plant leaves

Tree line

The highest point on a mountain at which trees can grow

Tropical

Relating to frost-free regions that have temperatures high enough to support year-round plant growth

Understory

An underlying layer of vegetation, especially the trees and shrubs between the forest canopy and the ground cover

Vertebrate

Animal with a backbone

Weed

A plant that grows where people do not want it to grow

Wind-pollination

The transfer of pollen by air from the male part of one seed plant to the female part of another

Whorl

A circle of leaves or flower parts

Further Research

General

...len, M. and Peisset, M. *Dangerous Animals*. New York: Chelsea House, 1992.

...ttenborough, D. *The Trials of Life*. Boston: Little, Brown, and Co., 1991.

...enyus, J. M. *Beastly Behaviors*. Reading, Massachusetts: Addison-Wesley Publishing Co., 1992.

...ulloch, D. K. *The Underwater Naturalist*. New York: Lyons & Burford, 1991.

...urne, D. *Dictionary of Nature*. New York: Dorling Kindersley, 1994.

...hinnery, M. *The Kingfisher Encyclopedia of Animals*. New York: Kingfisher, 1992.

...oleman, N. *Encyclopedia of Marine Animals*. New York: HarperCollins, 1991.

...he Concise Dictionary of Zoology. Edited by M. Allaby. New York: Oxford University Press, 1992.

...ncyclopedia of Life Sciences. 11 volumes. Edited by A. O'Daly. New York: Marshall Cavendish Corporation, 1996.

...ndangered! 18 volumes. New York: Marshall Cavendish Corporation, 1996-.

...leisher, P. *Webs of Life*. 4 volumes. New York: Marshall Cavendish Corporation, 1998.

...rzimek, B. *Grzimek's Animal Life Encyclopedia*. Volume 1. New York: McGraw-Hill, 1990.

...lessop, N. M. *Zoology: The Animal Kingdom. A Complete Course in 1000 Questions and Answers*. New York; McGraw-Hill, 1993.

...arade of Life: Monerans, Protists, Fungi, and Plants. Edited by A. Maton. Englewood Cliffs, New Jersey: Prentice-Hall, 1994.

Matthiessen, P. *Wildlife in America*. Revised edition. New York: Penguin Books, 1995.

Pringle, L. *Animal Monsters*. New York: Marshall Cavendish Corporation, 1997.

Biomes

Aldis, R. *Polar Lands*. New York: Dillon Press, 1992.

Amset, S. *Mountains*. Austin, Texas: Raintree/Steck Vaughn, 1993.

Biomes of the World. 10 volumes. New York: Marshall Cavendish Corporation, 1996.

Brinson, M., Brown, S., and Lugo, A. E. *Forested Wetlands*. New York: Elsevier, 1990.

Collinson, A. *Grassland*. New York: Dillon Press, 1992.

Goulding, M. "Flooded Forests of the Amazon." *Scientific American*, **268**, March 1993.

Lowell, W. A. *Urban Wildlife Habitats*. Minneapolis: University of Minnesota Press, 1994.

Moffett, M. W. *The High Frontier: Exploring the Tropical Rainforest Canopy*. Cambridge, Massachusetts: Harvard University Press, 1993.

Sayre, A. P. *Taiga*. New York: Twenty-First Century Books, 1994.

Thorne-Miller, B. and Catena, J. *The Living Ocean: Understanding and Protecting Marine Biodiversity*. Washington, DC: Island Press, 1991.

Wetlands: A Threatened Landscape. Edited by M. Williams. Boston: Blackwell Scientific Publications, 1991.

Invertebrates

Alderton, D. *A Step-by-Step Book About Stick Insects*. Neptune City, New Jersey: T.F.H. Publications, 1992.

Cornett, J. W. *Scorpions: Answers to Frequently Asked Questions*. Palm Springs: Palm Springs Desert Museum, 1992.

Dewey, J. O. *Bedbugs in Our House*. New York: Marshall Cavendish Corporation, 1997.

Dolling, W. R. *The Hemiptera*. New York: Natural History Museum Publications, Oxford University Press, 1991.

Facklam, H. *Insects*. New York: Twenty-First Century Books, 1994.

Fichter, G. S. *Bees, Wasps, and Ants*. New York: Golden Book, 1993.

Gerhold, J. E. *Beetles*. Edina: Abdo and Daughters, 1995.

Gibbons, G. *Spiders*. New York: Holiday House, 1993.

Holldober, B. and Wilson, E. O. *Journey to the Ants: A Story of Scientific Exploration*. Cambridge, Massachusetts: Harvard University Press, 1994.

Hunt, J. P. *Insects*. Morristown, New York: Silver Burdett Press, 1994.

Imes, R. *The Practical Entomologist*. New York: Simon & Schuster, 1992.

Julivert, A. *The Fascinating World of Beetles*. Hauppauge: Barron's, 1995.

Mound, L. *Eyewitness Guides: Insect*. New York: Alfred A. Knopf Inc., 1990.

O'Toole, C. *Encyclopedia of Insects and Spiders*. New York: Facts on File, 1990.

Parsons, A. *Amazing Spiders*. New York: Alfred A. Knopf Inc., 1990.

Fishes

Bailey, J. *Fish*. New York: Facts on File, 1990.

Cerullo, M. M. *Sharks: Challengers of the Deep*. New York: Cobblehill Books, 1993.

Lythgoe, J. and G. *Fishes of the Sea*. Boston: The M.I.T. Press, 1991

Michael, S. W. *Reef Sharks and Rays of the World*. Monterey: Sea Challengers, 1993.

Parker, S. *Fish*. New York: Alfred A. Knopf Inc., 1990.

Amphibians and Reptiles

Amphibians and Reptiles. Edited by P. E. Moler. Gainseville, Florida: University Press of Florida, 1992.

Anderson, E. G. *Annotated Molluskan Checklist*. Baton Rouge, Louisiana: Louisiana Geological Survey, 1993.

Collard, S. B. *Sea Snakes*. New York: St Martin's Press, 1993.

Ernst, C. H. *Venomous Reptiles of North America*. Washington, DC: Smithsonian Institution Publications, 1992.

Harris, V. A. *Sessile Animals of the Seashore*. New York: Chapman & Hall, 1990.

Lohmann, K. J. "How Sea Turtles Navigate." *Scientific American*, **226**, Jan. 1992

Martin, J. *Gila Monsters and Mexican Beaded Lizards*. Minneapolis: Capstone Press, 1995.

Parsons, A. *Amazing Snakes*. New York: Alfred A. Knopf Inc., 1990.

Reptiles and Amphibians. Edited by H. G. Cogger and R. G. Zweifel. New York: Smithmark, 1992.

Stokes, D. W. and L. Q. *A Guide to Amphibians and Reptiles.* Boston: Little, Brown, and Co., 1990.

Birds

Alcorn, G. *Birds and Their Young: Courtship, Nesting, Hatching, Fledging, and the Reproductive Cycle.* Harrisburg: Stackpole Books, 1991.

Berthold, P. *Bird Migration: A General Survey.* New York: Oxford University Press, 1993.

Brust, B. W. *Seabirds.* Mankato: Creative Education, 1991.

Clements, J. F. *Birds of the World: A Checklist.* USA: Ibis Publishing Co., 1991.

Gill, F. B. *Ornithology.* New York: W.H. Freeman and Company, 1990.

Kerlinger, J. K. *How Birds Migrate.* Mechanicsburg, Pennsylvania: Stackpole Books, 1995.

Laycock, G. *The Bird Watcher's Bible.* New York: Doubleday, 1994.

Monroe, B. L. and Sibley, C. G. *A World Checklist of Birds.* New Haven: Yale University Press, 1993.

Orr, R. and Taylor, B. *The Bird Atlas.* New York: Dorling Kindersley, 1993.

Shaw, F. *Birds of Eastern North America.* New York: Smithmark, 1990.

Shaw, F. *Birds of Western North America.* New York: Smithmark, 1990.

Terres, J. K. *Songbirds in Your Garden.* Chapel Hill: Algonquin Books, 1994.

Mammals

Barkausen, A. and Geiser, F. *Rabbits and Hares.* Milwaukee: Gareth Stevens, 1994.

Blum, D. *The Monkey Wars.* New York: Oxford University Press, 1994.

Burton, J. A. *Mammals of North America.* New York: Smithmark, 1991.

Connor, R. C. and Peterson, D. *The Lives of Whales and Dolphins.* New York: Henry Holt and Company, 1994.

Darling, J. and Nicklin, F. *With the Whales.* Minocqua, Wisconsin: NorthWord Press, 1990.

Encyclopedia of Mammals. Edited by A. Brown. New York: Marshall Cavendish Corporation, 1997.

Fenton, M. B. *Bats.* New York: Facts on File, 1992.

Kirkwood, J. K. *Biology, Rearing, and Care of Young Primates.* New York: Oxford University Press, 1992.

Moss, C. *Echo of the Elephants,* New York: WIlliam Morrow & Company, 1992.

Napier, J. R. and D. H. *The Natural History of the Primates.* Cambridge, Massachusetts: The M.I.T. Press, 1994.

Norris, K. S. and Pryir, K. *Dolphin Societies: Discoveries and Puzzles.* Berkeley, California: University of California Press, 1991.

Nowak, R. M. *Walker's Bats of the World.* Baltimore: John Hopkins University Press, 1994.

Nowak, R. M. *Walker's Mammals of the World.* 2 volumes. 5th edition. Baltimore: John Hopkins University Press, 1991.

Tibbitts, A. *African Rhinos.* Mankato: Capstone Press, 1992.

Plants and other organisms

Ahmadjian, V. *The Lichen Symbiosis.* New York: John Wiley & Sons, 1993.

Allen, M. and Peisset, M. *Dangerous Plants and Mushrooms.* New York, 1993.

Bell, P. *Green Plants: Their Origin and Diversity.* Portland, Oregon: Dioscorides Press, 1992.

Bennett, P. *Pollinating a Flower.* New York: Thomson Learning, 1994.

Capon, B. *Plant Survival: Adapting to a Hostile World.* Portland, Oregon: Timber Press, 1994.

Dowden, A. O. T. *The Blossom on the Bough: A Book of Trees.* New York: Ticknor and Fields, 1994.

Flowering Plants of the World. Edited by V. H. Heywood. New York: Oxford University Press, 1993.

Greenaway, T. *Mosses and Liverworts.* Austin, Texas: Raintree/Steck-Vaughn, 1992.

Heller, R. *Plants That Never Ever Bloom.* New York: Grosset & Dunlap, 1992.

Matthew, B. *The Complete Book of Bulbs, Corms, Tubers and Rhizomes.* Pleasantville: Reader's Digest Association, 1994.

Plant Life. Edited by D. M. Moore. New York: Oxford University Press, 1991.

Zomlefer, W. B. *Guide to Flowering Plant Families.* Chapel Hill: University of North Carolina Press, 1994.

OTHER USEFUL RESOURCES

MAGAZINES

Discover
P.O. Box 37823
Boone, Iowa 50037-0283

International Wildlife
8925 Leesburg Pike
Vienna, Virginia 22184

Natural History
American Museum of Natural History
Central Park West at 79th Street
New York, New York 10024

Scientific American
415 Madison Avenue
New York, New York 10017

Wildlife Conservation Magazine
WCS/Bronx Zoo
2300 Southern Boulevard
Bronx, New York 10460

INTERESTING PLACES TO VISIT

American Museum of Natural History
Central Park West at 79th Street
New York, New York 10024
Tel: (212) 769-5000

Denver Museum of Natural History
2001 Colorado Boulevard
Denver, Colorado 80205
Tel: (303) 370-6357

Field Museum of Natural History
Roosevelt Road at Lake Shore Drive
Chicago, Illinois 60605
Tel: (312) 922-9410

Monterey Bay Aquarium
886 Cannery Row
Monterey, California 93940
Tel: (408) 648-4888

National Museum of Natural History
Smithsonian Institution
Constitution Avenue at 10th Street
Washington, DC 20560
Tel: (202) 357-2700

New York Botanical Garden
Southern Boulevard and 200th Street
Bronx, New York 10458-5126
Tel: (718) 817-8700

Wildlife Conservation Society/Bronx Zoo
2300 Southern Boulevard
Bronx, New York 10460
Tel: (718) 220-5100

Geographic Index

AFRICA

Acacia **1**:16–17
African buffalo **1**:18–19
African wild dog **1**:20–21
Antelope **1**:42–43
Baboon **1**:54–55
Badger **1**:60–61
Bee-eater **2**:90–91
Camel **3**:142–145
Chameleon **3**:160–161
Cheetah **3**:164–165
Chimpanzee **3**:168–169
Cobra **3**:180–181
Colobus monkey **4**:200–201
Crocodile **4**:226–227
Dik-dik **4**:252–253
Eagle **5**:278–281
Elephant **5**:292–295
Elephant shrew **5**:296–297
Flamingo **5**:314–315
Flying fox **6**:328–329
Frog **6**:340–343
Gazelle **6**:352–353
Giraffe **6**:364–365
Heron **7**:424–425
Hippopotamus **7**:428–429
Honeyguide **7**:432–433
Hornbill **7**:434–435
Horse **7**:438–441
Hyena **8**:456–457
Hyrax **8**:458–459
Jackal **8**:472–473
Kestrel **8**:484–485
Leopard **9**:518–519
Lion **9**:528–529
Lungfish **9**:540–541
Mangrove **9**:552–553
Mongoose **10**:584–585
Monitor **10**:586–587
Mouse **10**:600–603
Mudskipper **10**:604–605
Nightingale **10**:612–613
Ostrich **11**:660–661
Oxpecker **11**:668–669
Pangolin **11**:674–675
Parrot **11**:676–677
Porcupine **12**:720–721
Python **12**:742–743
Rhinoceros **13**:776–779
Rubber tree **13**:788–789
Ruff **13**:790–791
Secretary bird **13**:814–815
Sesame **13**:818–819
Shoebill **13**:824–825
Sparrow **14**:852–853
Sparrow hawk **14**:854–855
Sunbird **14**:886–887
Vulture **16**:968–969
Warthog **16**:976–977
Wildebeest **16**:1004–1005
Zebra **16**:1022–1023

AFRICA, CENTRAL

Aardvark **1**:14–15
African buffalo **1**:18–19
African wild dog **1**:20–21
Baboon **1**:54–55
Bamboo **1**:62–63
Dik-dik **4**:252–253
Gorilla **6**:376–377
Lungfish **9**:540–541
Mandrill **9**:550–551
Monitor **10**:586–587
Nightingale **10**:612–613
Okapi **10**:636–637
Peacock **11**:680–681
Perch **11**:688–689
Shoebill **13**:824–825
Tenrec **15**:918–919

AFRICA, EASTERN

Aardvark **1**:14–15
African buffalo **1**:18–19
African wild dog **1**:20–21
Avocado **1**:48–49
Baboon **1**:54–55
Bee-eater **2**:90–91
Chameleon **3**:160–161
Chimpanzee **3**:168–169
Dik-dik **4**:252–253
Eland **5**:290–291
Elephant **5**:292–295
Elephant shrew **5**:296–297
Eucalyptus **5**:302–303
Gazelle **6**:352–353
Giraffe **6**:364–365
Ibex **8**:460–461
Impala **8**:466–467
Jackal **8**:472–473
Lungfish **9**:540–541
Monitor **10**:586–587
Oryx **11**:656–657
Perch **11**:688–689
Rhinoceros **13**:776–779
Shoebill **13**:824–825
Strawberry **14**:878–879
Sunbird **14**:886–887
Warthog **16**:976–977
Wildebeest **16**:1004–1005
Zebra **16**:1022–1023

AFRICA, NORTHERN

Aloe **1**:28–29
Arum **1**:46–47
Barbary ape **2**:72–73
Bee-eater **2**:90–91
Camel **3**:142–145
Cattail **3**:156–157
Deadly nightshade **4**:240–241
Donkey **5**:264–265
Dove **5**:268–269
Dragonfly **5**:270–271
Hemlock **7**:420–421
Hyena **8**:456–457
Kingfisher **8**:488–489
Mustard **10**:610–611
Oak **10**:624–625
Olive **10**:638–639
Palm **11**:670–671
Pine **11**:694–695
Poppy **12**:718–719
Rhinoceros **13**:776–779
Rose **13**:786–787
Weasel **16**:984–985
Wild cat **16**:1002–1003

AFRICA, SOUTHERN
(See also **MADAGASCAR**)

Aardvark **1**:14–15
African buffalo **1**:18–19
African wild dog **1**:20–21
Avocado **1**:48–49
Baboon **1**:54–55
Bee-eater **2**:90–91
Bird-of-paradise flower **2**:100–101
Bustard **2**:126–127
Dik-dik **4**:252–253
Eland **5**:290–291
Elephant **5**:292–295
Galago **6**:348–349
Hyena **8**:456–457
Hyrax **8**:458–459
Ibis **8**:462–463
Impala **8**:466–467
Jackal **8**:472–473
Meerkat **9**:562–563
Monitor **10**:586–587
Olive **10**:638–639
Oryx **11**:656–657
Puffer fish **12**:736–737
Rhinoceros **13**:776–779
Secretary bird **13**:814–815
Sesame **13**:818–819
Spider plant **14**:860–861
Springbok **14**:862–863
Strawberry **14**:878–879
Sugarcane **14**:884–885
Sunbird **14**:886–887
Warthog **16**:976–977
Weaver **16**:986–987
Weltwischia **16**:988–989
Wildebeest **16**:1004–1005
Zebra **16**:1022–1023

Figures in **boldface type** indicate volume numbers

AMERICA, CENTRAL

Acacia 1:16–17
Alligator 1:26–27
Anaconda 1:32–33
Anteater 1:40–41
Armadillo 1:44–45
Avocado 1:48–49
Axolotl 1:52–53
Bamboo 1:62–63
Cactus 3:138–139
Coffee 4:198–199
Crane 4:220–221
Crocodile 4:226–227
Deer 4:242–245
Flying squirrel 6:332–333
Frog 6:340–343
Gallinule 6:350–351
Gecko 6:354–355
Heron 7:424–425
Hummingbird 7:446–447
Ibis 8:462–463
Iguana 8:464–465
Jacana 8:470–471
Killdeer 8:486–487
Macaw 9:544–545
Mouse 10:600–603
Ocelot 10:632–633
Opossum 11:646–647
Oriole 11:652–653
Oropendola 11:654–655
Otter 11:662–663
Passionflower 11:678–679
Peccary 11:682–683
Pelican 11:684–685
Pine 11:694–695
Pocket gopher 12:712–713
Prairie dog 12:728–729
Puma 12:740–741
Quail 12:744–745
Quetzal 12:746–747
Raccoon 12:752–753
Rattlesnake 12:762–763
Raven 12:764–765
Roadrunner 13:782–783
Robin 13:784–785
Sea lion 13:810–811
Sesame 13:818–819
Sloth 14:844–845
Stork 14:876–877
Tapir 15:906–907

Viper 15:958–959
Vulture 16:968–969
Woodpecker 16:1014–1015
Yucca 16:1020–1021

AMERICA, NORTH

Acacia 1:16–17
Alligator 1:26–27
Antelope 1:42–43
Armadillo 1:44–45
Arum 1:46–47
Avocado 1:48–49
Avocet 1:50–51
Axolotl 1:52–53
Badger 1:60–61
Bamboo 1:62–63
Bass 2:76–77
Bat 2:78–81
Bear 2:82–85
Beaver 2:86–87
Bighorn sheep 2:94–95
Birch 2:96–97
Blackbird 2:102–103
Black widow spider 2:106–107
Bluebird 2:110–111
Blue jay 2:112–113
Bobcat 2:114–115
Buffalo 2:124–125
Butterfly 3:134–137
Cactus 3:138–139
Cardinal 3:148–149
Caribou 3:150–151
Carp 3:152–153
Catfish 3:154–155
Cattail 3:156–157
Chickadee 3:166–167
Chipmunk 3:170–171
Club moss 3:178–179
Condor 4:202–203
Coot 4:204–205
Cotton 4:214–215
Coyote 4:216–217
Crane 4:220–221
Crocodile 4:226–227
Crow 4:228–229

Curlew 4:234–235
Deer 4:242–245
Dove 5:268–269
Dragonfly 5:270–271
Duck 5:272–275
Eagle 5:278–281
Elk 5:298–299
Falcon 5:304–305
Ferret 5:308–309
Fig 5:310–311
Firefly 5:312–313
Flying squirrel 6:332–333
Fox 6:334–335
Foxglove 6:336–337
Frog 6:340–343
Gila monster 6:360–361
Ginkgo 6:362–363
Goat 6:368–369
Goldfinch 6:370–371
Goose 6:372–375
Grackle 6:378–379
Grape 6:380–381
Grebe 7:394–395
Groundhog 7:396–397
Grouse 7:400–401
Gull 7:404–405
Hare 7:412–413
Hawk 7:414–415
Heather 7:416–417
Holly 7:430–431
Horse 7:438–441
Horseshoe crab 7:442–443
Horsetail 7:444–445
Hummingbird 7:446–447
Ibis 8:462–463
Iguana 8:464–465
Jacana 8:470–471
Jellyfish 8:476–477
Kangaroo rat 8:480–481
Kestrel 8:484–485
Killdeer 8:486–487
Larch 8:506–507
Lemming 8:508–509
Lily 9:522–523
Limpkin 9:526–527
Loon 9:538–539
Lynx 9:542–543

Magnolia 9:546–547
Mangrove 9:552–553
Maple tree 9:554–555
Merganser 9:564–565
Millipede 9:566–567
Mink 9:570–571
Mistletoe 9:572–573
Mockingbird 9:574–575
Mole 10:582–583
Moose 10:588–589
Mouse 10:600–603
Musk ox 10:606–607
Muskrat 10:608–609
Mustard 10:610–611
Nuthatch 10:620–621
Ocelot 10:632–633
Olive 10:638–639
Opossum 11:646–647
Oriole 11:652–653
Otter 11:662–663
Owl 11:664–667
Palm 11:670–671
Parrot 11:676–677
Peccary 11:682–683
Pelican 11:684–685
Perch 11:688–689
Pine marten 11:696–697
Pitcher plant 11:702–703
Pocket gopher 12:712–713
Poppy 12:718–719
Porcupine 12:720–721
Potato 12:724–725
Prairie chicken 12:726–727
Prairie dog 12:728–729
Ptarmigan 12:734–735
Puffer fish 12:736–737
Puffin 12:738–739
Puma 12:740–741
Quail 12:744–745
Quillwort 12:748–749
Rabbit 12:750–751
Raccoon 12:752–753
Rattlesnake 12:762–763
Raven 12:764–765
Rice 13:780–781
Roadrunner 13:782–783
Robin 13:784–785
Salamander 13:794–795

Figures in **boldface type** indicate volume numbers

Sambar **13**:798–799
Scorpion **13**:800–801
Sea horse **13**:806–807
Seal **13**:808–809
Sequoia **13**:816–817
Sesame **13**:818–819
Shrew **13**:826–827
Sidewinder **13**:830–831
Skunk **14**:842–843
Soybean **14**:850–851
Spider **14**:856–859
Squash **14**:864–865
Squirrel **14**:868–869
Starling **14**:872–873
Stork **14**:876–877
Strawberry **14**:878–879
Sugarcane **14**:884–885
Swallow **14**:890–891
Swan **14**:892–893
Swift **14**:894–895
Tarantula **15**:908–909
Terrapin **15**:924–925
Toad **15**:930–931
Tomato **15**:932–933
Tortoise **15**:934–935
Trout **15**:940–941
Turkey **15**:946–947
Turtle **15**:948–949
Venus flytrap **15**:956–957
Viper **15**:958–959
Vole **16**:966–967
Vulture **16**:968–969
Water lily **16**:980–981
Water moccasin
 16:982–983
Weasel **16**:984–985
Wolf **16**:1008–1011
Woodpecker
 16:1014–1015
Yucca **16**:1020–1021

MERICA, SOUTH
Alligator **1**:26–27
Anaconda **1**:32–33
Anteater **1**:40–41
Armadillo **1**:44–45
Avocado **1**:48–49
Avocet **1**:50–51
Bamboo **1**:62–63

Bat **2**:78–81
Bear **2**:82–85
Brazil nut tree **2**:120–121
Bromeliad **2**:122–123
Capybara **3**:146–147
Catfish **3**:154–155
Cinchona **3**:174–175
Coffee **4**:198–199
Condor **4**:202–203
Coot **4**:204–205
Crocodile **4**:226–227
Deer **4**:242–245
Flamingo **5**:314–315
Frog **6**:340–343
Gallinule **6**:350–351
Gecko **6**:354–355
Guinea pig **7**:402–403
Heron **7**:424–425
Horse **7**:438–441
Hummingbird **7**:446–447
Iguana **8**:464–465
Jaguar **8**:474–475
Killdeer **8**:486–487
Kingfisher **8**:488–489
Limpkin **9**:526–527
Llama **9**:534–535
Lungfish **9**:540–541
Macaw **9**:544–545
Mangrove **9**:552–553
Marmoset **9**:558–559
Mimosa **9**:568–569
Mouse **10**:600–603
Mustard **10**:610–611
Night monkey
 10:614–615
Nutria **10**:622–623
Ocelot **10**:632–633
Olive **10**:638–639
Oropendola **11**:654–655
Otter **11**:662–663
Parrot **11**:676–677
Passionflower **11**:678–679
Peccary **11**:682–683
Penguin **11**:686–687
Piranha **11**:700–701
Pitcher plant **11**:702–703
Porcupine **12**:720–721

Potato **12**:724–725
Puma **12**:740–741
Quail **12**:744–745
Raccoon **12**:752–753
Rhea **13**:774–775
Rice **13**:780–781
Rubber tree **13**:788–789
Sea lion **13**:810–811
Sesame **13**:818–819
Sloth **14**:844–845
Stork **14**:876–877
Sugarcane **14**:884–885
Sunflower **14**:888–889
Tamarin **15**:904–905
Tapir **15**:906–907
Tomato **15**:932–933
Toucan **15**:936–937
Uakari **15**:952–953
Viper **15**:958–959
Vulture **16**:968–969
Water lily **16**:980–981

**ANTARCTIC (seas, ice,
and land)**
 Penguin **11**:686–687
 Seal **13**:808–809
 Tern **15**:922–923

ARABIAN PENINSULA
(See also **MIDDLE EAST**)
 Aloe **1**:28–29
 Baboon **1**:54–55
 Cheetah **3**:164–165
 Donkey **5**:264–265
 Ibex **8**:460–461
 Oryx **11**:656–657
 Wolf **16**:1008–1011

**ARCTIC (ocean, land,
and ice caps)**
 Polar bear **12**:714–715
 Seal **13**:808–809
 Sturgeon **14**:880–881
 Swan **14**:892–893
 Tern **15**:922–923
 Vole **16**:966–967
 Walrus **16**:974–975

ASIA (See also **CHINA;
EURASIA; JAPAN**)
 Avocet **1**:50–51
 Bee-eater **2**:90–91
 Blackbuck **2**:104–105
 Camel **3**:142–145
 Chameleon **3**:160–161
 Club moss **3**:178–179
 Coffee **4**:198–199
 Deadly nightshade
  4:240–241
 Deer **4**:242–245
 Dhole **4**:250–251
 Donkey **5**:264–265
 Elephant **5**:292–295
 Flying fox **6**:328–329
 Flying squirrel **6**:332–333
 Fox **6**:334–335
 Gecko **6**:354–355
 Gerbil **6**:356–357
 Gibbon **6**:358–359
 Goat **6**:368–369
 Hamster **7**:410–411
 Hare **7**:412–413
 Heather **7**:416–417
 Hemlock **7**:420–421
 Heron **7**:424–425
 Hornbill **7**:434–435
 Horse **7**:438–441
 Horsetail **7**:444–445
 Ibex **8**:460–461
 Leopard **9**:518–519
 Loon **9**:538–539
 Merganser **9**:564–565
 Millipede **9**:566–567
 Mistletoe **9**:572–573
 Mouse **10**:600–603
 Mustard **10**:610–611
 Nightingale **10**:612–613
 Panda **11**:672–673
 Pangolin **11**:674–675
 Passionflower **11**:678–679
 Pheasant **11**:692-693
 Pine **11**:694–695
 Pitcher plant **11**:702–703
 Poppy **12**:718–719
 Potato **12**:724–725
 Puffer fish **12**:736–737
 Python **12**:742–743
 Rhinoceros **13**:776–779

Figures in **boldface type** indicate volume numbers

Rice 13:780–781
Rose 13:786–787
Ruff 13:790–791
Silkworm 14:838–839
Sparrow 14:852–853
Sparrow hawk 14:854–855
Squash 14:864–865
Sunflower 14:888–889
Swallow 14:890–891
Trout 15:940–941
Viper 15:958–959
Vole 16:966–967
Weasel 16:984–985
Weaver 16:986–987
Wild cat 16:1002–1003
Wolf 16:1008–1011
Yak 16:1018–1019

ASIA, NORTHERN
Bear 2:82–85
Curlew 4:234–235
Gerbil 6:356–357
Gull 7:404–405
Wolf 16:1008–1011

ASIA, SOUTHEAST
(including INDONESIA)
Badger 1:60–61
Bamboo 1:62–63
Bear 2:82–85
Bee-eater 2:90–91
Cobra 3:180–181
Flying lemur 6:330–331
Gecko 6:354–355
Gibbon 6:358–359
Komodo dragon
  8:494–495
Leopard 9:518–519
Monitor 10:586–587
Mouse 10:600–603
Orangutan 11:648–649
Peacock 11:680–681
Pine 11:694–695
Proboscis monkey
  12:732–733
Python 12:742–743
Rafflesia 12:754–755
Rice 13:781–782
Rubber tree 13:788–789
Sambar 13:798–799

Soybean 14:850–851
Tapir 15:906–907
Tiger 15:928–929
Water lily 16:980–981

ASIA, SOUTHERN
(including INDIA)
Badger 1:60–61
Bear 2:82–85
Bee-eater 2:90–91
Blackbuck 2:104–105
Cobra 3:180–181
Cotton 4:214–215
Deer 4:242–245
Dormouse 5:266–267
Dove 5:268–269
Elephant 5:292–295
Fig 5:310–311
Flamingo 5:314–315
Flying squirrel 6:332–333
Gecko 6:354–355
Gerbil 6:356–357
Gibbon 6:358–359
Gnetophyte 6:366–367
Honeyguide 7:432–433
Hyena 8:456–457
Jackal 8:472–473
Lion 9:528–529
Mongoose 10:584–585
Nilgai 10:616–617
Olive 10:638–639
Peacock 11:680–681
Poppy 12:718–719
Porcupine 12:720–721
Rice 13:780–781
Rose 13:786–787
Sambar 13:798–799
Sesame 13:818–819
Soybean 14:850–851
Sugarcane 14:884–885
Tea 15:912–913
Tiger 15:928–929
Water lily 16:980–981

ATLANTIC OCEAN
Albatross 1:22–23
Angler fish 1:36–37

Cod 3:188–189
Eel 5:288–289
Flying fish 6:326–327
Frigate bird 6:338–339
Gull 7:404–405
Halibut 7:408–409
Herring 7:426–427
Horseshoe crab 7:442–443
Lamprey 8:504–505
Lobster 9:536–537
Manatee 9:548–549
Mudskipper 10:604–605
Pipefish 11:698–699
Porpoise 12:722–723
Ray 12:766–767
Salmon 13:796–797
Sea urchin 13:812–813
Shrimp 13:828–829
Skua 14:840–841
Squid 14:866–867
Sturgeon 14:880–881

AUSTRALIA
Acacia 1:16–17
Avocado 1:48–49
Banksia 2:70–71
Bee-eater 2:90–91
Bird of paradise 2:98–99
Bowerbird 2:118–119
Clam 3:176–177
Cockatoo 3:182–183
Crocodile 4:226–227
Dingo 4:254–255
Echidna 5:286–287
Emu 5:300–301
Eucalyptus 5:302–303
Gecko 6:354–355
Gunn's bandicoot
  7:406–407
Horse 7:438–441
Kangaroo 8:478–479
Kingfisher 8:488–489
Koala 8:492–493
Kookaburra 8:496–497
Lungfish 9:540–541
Marsupial mole
  9:560–561

Monitor 10:586–587
Mouse 10:600–603
Numbat 10:618–619
Olive 10:638–639
Passionflower
  11:678–679
Pitcher plant 11:702–70
Platypus 12:710–711
Puffer fish 12:736–737
Ruff 13:790–791
Sambar 13:798–799
Sea lion 13:810–811
Strawberry 14:878–879
Sugarcane 14:884–885
Swan 14:892–893
Tasmanian devil
  15:910–911
Tree kangaroo
  15:938–939
Wallaby 16:972–973
Wombat 16:1012–1013

CARIBBEAN ISLANDS
AND CARIBBEAN SEA
Acacia 1:16–17
Anaconda 1:32–33
Avocado 1:48–49
Coot 4:204–205
Coral 4:206–209
Frog 6:340–343
Gallinule 6:350–351
Iguana 8:464–465
Killdeer 8:486–487
Limpkin 9:526–527
Lobster 9:536–537
Manatee 9:548–549
Mangrove 9:552–553
Sea horse 13:806–807

CHINA
Alligator 1:26–27
Cotton 4:214–215
Deer 4:242–245
Gerbil 6:356–357
Ginkgo 6:362–363
Ibex 8:460–461
Panda 11:672–673
Peacock 11:680–681
Poppy 12:718–719
Sesame 13:818–819

Figures in **boldface type** indicate volume numbers

Silkworm **14**:838–839
Soybean **14**:850–851
Sunflower **14**:888–889
Tea **15**:912–913
Wolf **16**:1008–1011

▮URASIA
Avocet **1**:50–51
Cattail **3**:156–157
Chipmunk **3**:170–171
Dormouse **5**:266–267
Eagle **5**:278–281
Fox **6**:334–335
Goat **6**:368–369
Goose **6**:372–375
Grebe **7**:394–395
Kingfisher **8**:488–489
Lemming **8**:508–509
Lynx **9**:542–543
Moose **10**:588–589
Nuthatch **10**:620–621
Perch **11**:688–689
Pine **11**:694–695
Ptarmigan **12**:734–735
Raven **12**:764–765
Rose **13**:786–787
Ruff **13**:790–791
Saiga **13**:792–793
Sesame **13**:818–819
Starling **14**:872–873
Sunflower **14**:888–889
Vole **16**:966–967
Weasel **16**:984–985

▮UROPE
Avocet **1**:50–51
Bear **2**:82–85
Bee-eater **2**:90–91
Blue jay **2**:112–113
Caribou **3**:150–151
Carp **3**:152–153
Cattail **3**:156–157
Chamois **3**:162–163
Deadly nightshade
   4:240–241
Deer **4**:242–245
Dormouse **5**:266–267
Dragonfly **5**:270–271
Duck **5**:272–275
Earwig **5**:284–285

Elk **5**:298–299
Flying squirrel **6**:332–333
Fox **6**:334–335
Foxglove **6**:336–337
Ginkgo **6**:362–363
Goat **6**:368–369
Grape **6**:380–381
Hamster **7**:410–411
Hare **7**:412–413
Heather **7**:416–417
Hedgehog **7**:418–419
Hemlock **7**:420–421
Holly **7**:430–431
Horse **7**:438–441
Horsetail **7**:444–445
Kestrel **8**:484–485
Larch **8**:506–507
Loon **9**:538–539
Merganser **9**:564–565
Mink **9**:570–571
Mistletoe **9**:572–573
Mole **10**:582–583
Moose **10**:588–589
Mouse **10**:600–603
Musk ox **10**:606–607
Muskrat **10**:608–609
Mustard **10**:610–611
Nuthatch **10**:620–621
Perch **11**:688–689
Pine **11**:694–695
Pine marten
   11:696–697
Poppy **12**:718–719
Porcupine **12**:720–721
Potato **12**:724–725
Puffin **12**:738–739
Robin **13**:784–785
Rose **13**:786–787
Soybean **14**:850–851
Sparrow **14**:852–853
Sparrow hawk **14**:854–855
Squash **14**:864–865
Starling **14**:872–873
Stork **14**:876–877
Strawberry **14**:878–879
Sunflower **14**:888–889
Swallow **14**:890–891

Swan **14**:892–893
Tomato **15**:932–933
Trout **15**:940–941
Vole **16**:966–967
Water lily **16**:980–981
Weasel **16**:984–985
Wild cat **16**:1002–1003
Wolf **16**:1008–1011

EUROPE, EASTERN
Carp **3**:152–153
Hamster **7**:410–411
Wolf **16**:1008–1011

EUROPE, NORTHERN
Caribou **3**:150–151
Cuckoo **4**:230–231
Curlew **4**:234–235
Deer **4**:242–245
Dove **5**:268–269
Eagle **5**:278–281
Goose **6**:372–375
Gull **7**:404–405
Larch **8**:506–507
Ruff **13**:790–791
Wolf **16**:1008–1011

EUROPE, SOUTHERN
Bee-eater **2**:90–91
Chameleon **3**:160–161
Deer **4**:242–245
Dove **5**:268–269
Flamingo **5**:314–315
Gecko **6**:354–355
Jackal **8**:472–473
Lynx **9**:542–543
Nightingale **10**:612–613
Oak **10**:624–625

GALAPAGOS ISLANDS
Albatross **1**:22–23
Iguana **8**:464–465
Tortoise **15**:934–935

INDIAN OCEAN
Albatross **1**:22–23
Angelfish **1**:34–35

Coelacanth **3**:190–191
Dugong **5**:276–277
Eel **5**:288–289
Frigate bird **6**:338–339
Grouper **7**:398–399
Horseshoe crab
   7:442–443
Lionfish **9**:530–531
Mudskipper **10**:604–605
Sea urchin **13**:812–813
Wrasse **16**:1016–1017

JAPAN
Albatross **1**:22–23
Crane **4**:220–221
Cycad **4**:236–237
Ginkgo **6**:362–363
Rice **13**:780–781
Sesame **13**:818–819
Soybean **14**:850–851
Strawberry **14**:878–879
Tea **15**:912–913

MADAGASCAR
Bamboo **1**:62–63
Bee-eater **2**:90–91
Chameleon **3**:160–161
Lemur **8**:510–511
Mongoose **10**:584–585
Pitcher plant **11**:702–703
Rice **13**:780–781
Tenrec **15**:918–919

**MEDITERRANEAN
REGION**
Aloe **1**:28–29
Arum **1**:46–47
Bee-eater **2**:90–91
Chameleon **3**:160–161
Deer **4**:242–245
Dove **5**:268–269
Dugong **5**:276–277
Fig **5**:310–311
Flamingo **5**:314–315
Gecko **6**:354–355
Nightingale **10**:612–613
Olive **10**:638–639
Pipefish **11**:698–699
Poppy **12**:718–719
Sesame **13**:818–819

Figures in **boldface type** indicate volume numbers

MIDDLE EAST

Badger **1**:60–61
Camel **3**:142–145
Chameleon **3**:160–161
Cheetah **3**:164–165
Donkey **5**:264–265
Dove **5**:268–269
Dragonfly **5**:270–271
Gecko **6**:354–355
Gerbil **6**:356–357
Hamster **7**:410–411
Hyena **8**:456–457
Jackal **8**:472–473
Leopard **9**:518–519
Mongoose **10**:584–585
Nightingale **10**:612–613
Olive **10**:638–639
Palm **11**:670–671
Scorpion **13**:800–801
Sesame **13**:818–819

NEW GUINEA

Bee-eater **2**:90–91
Bird of paradise **2**:98–99
Bowerbird **2**:118–119
Cockatoo **3**:182–183
Echidna **5**:286–287
Gecko **6**:354–355
Tree kangaroo
   15:938–939
Wallaby **16**:972–973

NEW ZEALAND

Gecko **6**:354–355
Kiwi **8**:490–491
Kookaburra **8**:496–497
Mustard **10**:610–611
Potato **12**:724–725
Rose **13**:786–787
Sambar **13**:798–799
Sea lion **13**:810–811
Strawberry **14**:878–879

PACIFIC ISLANDS AND PACIFIC OCEAN

Albatross **1**:22–23
Angelfish **1**:34–35
Dugong **5**:276–277
Eel **5**:288–289
Flying fish **6**:326–327

Grouper **7**:398–399
Gull **7**:404–405
Herring **7**:426–427
Horseshoe crab
   7:442–443
Lionfish **9**:530–531
Manatee **9**:548–549
Mudskipper **10**:604–605
Otter **11**:662–663
Pipefish **11**:698–699
Porpoise **12**:722–723
Puffer fish **12**:736–737
Salmon **13**:796–797
Seal **13**:808–809
Sea lion **13**:810–811
Starfish **14**:870–871
Sturgeon **14**:880–881
Sugarcane **14**:884–885
Trout **15**:940–941
Wrasse **16**:1016–1017

WORLDWIDE DISTRIBUTION (Land)

Alga **1**:24–25
Amoeba **1**:30–31
Ant **1**:38–39
Bacterium **1**:56–59
Bat **2**:78–81
Bee **2**:88–89
Beetle **2**:92–93
Bladderwort **2**:108–109
Bonsai **2**:112–113
Butterfly **3**:134–135
Caddis fly **3**:140–141
Cockroach **3**:184–185
Corn **4**:212–213
Crab **4**:218–219
Crane **4**:220–221
Cranefly **4**:222–223
Cricket **4**:224–225
Dandelion **4**:238–239
Dove **5**:268–269
Earthworm **5**:282–283
Eel **5**:288–289
Falcon **5**:304–305
Fern **5**:306–307
Flea **5**:316–317

Fly **5**:318–319
Fungus **6**:344–347
Gallinule **6**:350–351
Grass **6**:382–383
Grasshopper **7**:390–391
Hornet **7**:436–437
Hydra **8**:454–455
Ladybug **8**:498–499
Lichen **9**:520–521
Liverwort **9**:532–533
Millipede **9**:566–567
Mosquito **10**:590–591
Moss **10**:592–593
Moth **10**:594–597
Mouse **10**:600–603
Orchid **11**:650–651
Osprey **11**:658–659
Otter **11**:662–663
Owl **11**:664–667
Praying mantis
   12:730–731
Rat **12**:760–761
Salamander **13**:794–795
Slug **14**:846–847
Snail **14**:848–849
Sparrow **14**:852–853
Spider **14**:856–859
Squirrel **14**:868–869
Stinging nettle
   14:874–875
Swift **14**:894–895
Toad **15**:930–931
Wasp **16**:978–979
Wheat **16**:998–999
Willow **16**:1006–1007

WORLDWIDE DISTRIBUTION (Oceans)

Alga **1**:24–25
Angler fish **1**:36–37
Barracuda **2**:74–75
Clam **3**:176–177
Coral **4**:206–209
Dolphin **5**:262–263
Hermit crab **7**:422–423
Jellyfish **8**:476–477
Lobster **9**:536–537

Marlin **9**:556–557
Ocean sunfish
   10:630–631
Octopus **10**:634–635
Petrel **11**:690–691
Sea anemone **13**:804–805
Sea horse **13**:806–807
Sea urchin **13**:812–813
Seaweed **8**:482–483
Shark **13**:820–823
Shrimp **13**:828–829
Squid **14**:866–867
Starfish **14**:870–871
Tuna **15**:942–943
Turtle **15**:948–951
Whale **16**:994–997

WORLDWIDE TROPICS AND SUBTROPICS

Cicada **3**:172–173
Coconut palm **3**:186–187
Cycad **4**:236–237
Flying fish **6**:326–327
Grasshopper **7**:390–391
Lime **9**:524–525
Parrot **11**:676–677
Praying mantis
   12:730–731
Scorpion **13**:800–801
Soybean **14**:850–851
Termite **15**:920–921
Tortoise **15**:934–935
Walking stick **16**:970–971
Whisk fern **16**:1000–1001

Figures in **boldface type** indicate volume numbers

Biomes Index

Biomes may be understood simply as regions of the earth that are differentiated by temperature and rainfall. Each biome contains a variety of climates, habitats, and organisms. The following index provides a general guide to articles on organisms associated with particular biomes, including organisms that live in or near water within each biome. Organisms that live in nearly every biome on earth are listed together under the first heading. Organisms that live in more than one biome may appear under more than one heading.

Organisms that live throughout the world

Ant 1:38–39
Bat 2:78–81
Bee 2:88–89
Beetle 2:92–93
Bladderwort 2:108–109
Butterfly 3:134–137
Caddis fly 3:140–141
Cattail 3:156–157
Cockroach 3:184–185
Cranefly 4:222–223
Cricket 4:224–225
Dove 5:268–269
Eagle 5:278–281
Earthworm 5:282–283
Falcon 5:304–305
Flea 5:316–317
Fly 5:318–319
Fungus 6:344–347
Gallinule 6:350–351
Grass 6:382–383
Grasshopper 7:390–391
Ladybug 8:498–499
Lichen 9:520–521
Liverwort 9:532–533
Millipede 9:566–567
Mosquito 10:590–591
Moss 10:592–593
Moth 10:594–597
Mouse 10:600–603
Mustard 10:610–611
Opossum 11:646–647
Owl 11:664–667
Poppy 12:718–719
Potato 12:724–725
Praying mantis 12:730–731
Rat 12:760–761

Raven 12:764–765
Rose 13:786–787
Silkworm 14:838–839
Skunk 14:842–843
Slug 14:846–847
Snail 14:848–849
Spider 14:856–859
Starling 14:872–873
Stinging nettle 14:874–875
Swallow 14:890–891
Swift 14:894–895
Tomato 15:932–933
Turtle 15:948–949
Vole 16:966–967
Vulture 16:968–969
Wasp 16:978–979
Wild cat 16:1002–1003
Wolf 16:1008–1011

Desert

Baboon 1:54–55
Bobcat 2:114–115
Cactus 3:138–139
Camel 3:142–145
Cheetah 3:164–165
Cicada 3:172–173
Cobra 3:180–181
Condor 4:202–203
Coot 4:204–205
Duck 5:272–275
Gecko 6:354–355
Gerbil 6:356–357
Heron 7:424–425
Hyrax 8:458–459
Ibis 8:462–463
Iguana 8:464–465

Kangaroo rat 8:480–481
Marsupial mole 9:560–561
Meerkat 9:562–563
Monitor 10:586–587
Palm 11:670–671
Puma 12:740–741
Roadrunner 13:782–783
Scorpion 13:800–801
Sidewinder 13:830–831
Tarantula 15:908–909
Welwitschia 16:988–989
Yucca 16:1020–1021

Grassland

Aardvark 1:14–15
Acacia 1:16–17
African buffalo 1:18–19
African wild dog 1:20–21
Anteater 1:40–41
Antelope 1:42–43
Armadillo 1:44–45
Arum 1:46–47
Avocet 1:50–51
Bass 2:76–77
Bee-eater 2:90–91
Blackbird 2:102–103
Black widow spider 2:106–107
Bobcat 2:114–115
Buffalo 2:124–125
Bustard 2:126–127
Carp 3:152–153
Catfish 3:154–155
Cheetah 3:164–165
Cicada 3:172–173
Coffee 4:198–199
Coot 4:204–205

Corn 4:212–213
Cotton 4:214–215
Coyote 4:216–217
Crane 4:220–221
Cuckoo 4:230–231
Curlew 4:234–235
Dandelion 4:238–239
Dingo 4:254–255
Duck 5:272–275
Echidna 5:286–287
Eland 5:290–291
Elephant 5:292–295
Ferret 5:308–309
Fox 6:334–335
Gazelle 6:352–353
Gecko 6:354–355
Giraffe 6:364–365
Goldfinch 6:370–371
Goose 6:372–375
Grackle 6:378–379
Grebe 7:394–395
Grouse 7:400–401
Gunn's bandicoot 7:406–407
Hamster 7:410–411
Heron 7:424–425
Hippopotamus 7:428–429
Honeyguide 7:432–433
Hornbill 7:434–435
Horse 7:438–441
Horsetail 7:444–445
Hummingbird 7:446–447
Hyena 8:456–457
Hyrax 8:458–459
Ibis 8:462–463
Iguana 8:464–465
Impala 8:466–467
Jackal 8:472–473
Kangaroo 8:478–479
Kestrel 8:484–485
Killdeer 8:486–487

Figures in **boldface type** indicate volume numbers

Kingfisher **8**:488–489
Komodo dragon
 8:494–495
Leopard **9**:518–519
Lily **9**:522–523
Limpkin **9**:526–527
Lion **9**:528–529
Llama **9**:534–535
Lungfish **9**:540–541
Meerkat **9**:562–563
Mink **9**:570–571
Mongoose **10**:584–585
Muskrat **10**:608–609
Nutria **10**:622–623
Oriole **11**:652–653
Osprey **11**:658–659
Ostrich **11**:660–661
Oxpecker **11**:668–669
Pelican **11**:684–685
Pheasant **11**:692–693
Pocket gopher
 12:712–713
Prairie chicken
 12:726–727
Prairie dog **12**:728–729
Puma **12**:740–741
Quail **12**:744–745
Rabbit **12**:750–751
Raccoon **12**:752–753
Rhea **13**:774–775
Rhinoceros **13**:776–779
Rice **13**:780–781
Ruff **13**:790–791
Saiga **13**:792–793
Secretary bird
 13:814–815
Sesame **13**:818–819
Shoebill **13**:824–825
Soybean **14**:850–851
Springbok **14**:862–863
Squash **14**:864–865
Stork **14**:876–877
Strawberry **14**:878–879
Sunflower **14**:888–889
Swan **14**:892–893
Termite **15**:920–921
Turkey **15**:946–947
Venus flytrap **15**:956–957
Warthog **16**:976–977
Water lily **16**:980–981

Water moccasin
 16:982–983
Weasel **16**:984–985
Wheat **16**:998–999
Wildebeest **16**:1004–1005
Wombat **16**:1012–1013
Zebra **16**:1022–1023

Ocean

Albatross **1**:22–23
Angelfish **1**:34–35
Angler fish **1**:36–37
Barracuda **2**:74–75
Bass **2**:76–77
Clam **3**:176–177
Cod **3**:188–189
Coelacanth **3**:190–191
Coral **4**:206–209
Crab **4**:218–219
Dolphin **5**:262–263
Dugong **5**:276–277
Eel **5**:288–289
Flying fish **6**:326–327
Frigate bird **6**:338–339
Grouper **7**:398–399
Gull **7**:404–405
Halibut **7**:408–409
Hermit crab **7**:422–423
Herring **7**:426–427
Horseshoe crab **7**:442–443
Jellyfish **8**:476–477
Kelp and other seaweeds
 8:482–483
Lamprey **8**:504–505
Lionfish **9**:530–531
Lobster **9**:536–537
Manatee **9**:548–549
Marlin **9**:556–557
Ocean sunfish **10**:630–631
Octopus **10**:634–635
Otter **11**:662–663
Pelican **11**:684–685
Penguin **11**:686–687
Petrel **11**:690–691
Pipefish **11**:698–699
Porpoise **12**:722–723

Puffer fish **12**:736–737
Puffin **12**:738–739
Ray **12**:766–767
Salmon **13**:796–797
Sea anemone **13**:804–805
Sea horse **13**:806–807
Seal **13**:808–809
Sea lion **13**:810–811
Sea urchin **13**:812–813
Shark **13**:820–823
Shrimp **13**:828–829
Skua **14**:840–841
Squid **14**:866–867
Starfish **14**:870–871
Sturgeon **14**:880–881
Tern **15**:922–923
Terrapin **15**:924–925
Toad **15**:930–931
Trout **15**:940–941
Tuna **15**:942–943
Walrus **16**:974–975
Whale **16**:994–997
Wrasse **16**:1016–1017

Rainforest

Alligator **1**:26–27
Anaconda **1**:32–33
Anteater **1**:40–41
Armadillo **1**:44–45
Avocado **1**:48–49
Avocet **1**:50–51
Bamboo **1**:62–63
Bear **2**:82–85
Bird of paradise **2**:98–99
Bowerbird **2**:118–119
Brazil nut tree
 2:120–121
Bromeliad **2**:122–123
Capybara **3**:146–147
Chameleon **3**:160–161
Chimpanzee **3**:168–169
Cicada **3**:172–173
Cinchona **3**:174–175
Cockatoo **3**:182–183
Coconut palm **3**:186–187
Coffee **4**:198–199

Colobus monkey
 4:200–201
Coot **4**:204–205
Crocodile **4**:226–227
Cycad **4**:236–237
Dhole **4**:250–251
Elephant **5**:292–295
Fern **5**:306–307
Flamingo **5**:314–315
Flying fox **6**:328–329
Flying lemur **6**:330–331
Frog **6**:340–343
Galago **6**:348–349
Gecko **6**:354–355
Gibbon **6**:358–359
Gnetophyte **6**:366–367
Gorilla **6**:376–377
Guinea pig **7**:402–403
Heron **7**:424–425
Hummingbird **7**:446–447
Ibis **8**:462–463
Iguana **8**:464–465
Jacana **8**:470–471
Jaguar **8**:474–475
Lemur **8**:510–511
Leopard **9**:518–519
Lime **9**:524–525
Limpkin **9**:526–527
Macaw **9**:544–545
Mandrill **9**:550–551
Mangrove **9**:552–553
Marmoset **9**:558–559
Mimosa **9**:568–569
Mudskipper **10**:604–605
Night monkey
 10:614–615
Ocelot **10**:632–633
Okapi **10**:636–637
Orangutan **11**:648–649
Orchid **11**:650–651
Oropendola **11**:654–655
Osprey **11**:658–659
Palm **11**:670–671
Parrot **11**:676–677
Passionflower **11**:678–679
Peacock **11**:680–681
Peccary **11**:682–683
Piranha **11**:700–701
Proboscis monkey
 12:732–733

Figures in **boldface type** indicate volume numbers

Puma **12**:740–741
Python **12**:742–743
Quetzal **12**:746–747
Rafflesia **12**:754–755
Rice **13**:780–781
Rubber tree **13**:786–789
Sloth **14**:844–845
Spider plant **14**:860–861
Sugarcane **14**:884–885
Tamarin **15**:904–905
Tapir **15**:906–907
Tarantula **15**:908–909
Tenrec **15**:918–919
Tiger **15**:928–929
Toucan **15**:936–937
Tree kangaroo
    15:938–939
Uakari **15**:952–953
Viper **15**:958–959
Walking stick **16**:970–971
Water lily **16**:980–981
Whisk fern **16**:1000–1001

Scrubland (or chaparral)

Aloe **1**:28–29
Antelope **1**:42–43
Baboon **1**:54–55
Banksia **2**:70–71
Barbary ape **2**:72–73
Bighorn sheep **2**:94–95
Bird-of-paradise flower
    2:100–101
Blackbuck **2**:104–105
Bobcat **2**:114–115
Buffalo **2**:124–125
Carp **3**:152–153
Chamois **3**:162–163
Cicada **3**:172–173
Cobra **3**:180–181
Condor **4**:202–203
Dik-dik **4**:252–253
Donkey **5**:264–265
Eland **5**:290–291
Elephant **5**:292–295
Elephant shrew **5**:296–297
Emu **5**:300–301
Fox **6**:334–335
Gila monster **6**:360–361

Grape **6**:380–381
Heather **7**:416–417
Ibex **6**:460–461
Lily **9**:522–523
Lime **9**:524–525
Llama **9**:534–535
Mongoose **10**:584–585
Monitor **10**:586–587
Numbat **10**:618–619
Olive **10**:638–639
Oryx **11**:656–657
Ostrich **11**:660–661
Pangolin **11**:674–675
Rattlesnake **12**:762–763
Sesame **13**:818–819
Sunbird **14**:886–887
Swan **14**:892–893
Tortoise **15**:934–935
Weaver **16**:986–987
Zebra **16**:1022–1023

Taiga

Bear **2**:82–85
Caribou **3**:150–151
Catfish **3**:154–155
Club moss **3**:178–179
Crane **4**:220–221
Elk **5**:298–299
Fox **6**:334–335
Grebe **7**:394–395
Horsetail **7**:444–445
Lamprey **8**:504–505
Lily **9**:522–523
Loon **9**:538–539
Lynx **9**:542–543
Merganser **9**:564–565
Mink **9**:570–571
Mole **10**:582–583
Moose **10**:588–589
Muskrat **10**:608–609
Osprey **11**:658–659
Otter **11**:662–663
Pine **11**:694–695
Pine marten **11**:696–697
Ruff **13**:790–791
Shrew **13**:826–827

Swan **14**:892–893
Water lily **16**:980–981
Weasel **16**:984–985

Temperate forest

Alligator **1**:26–27
Armadillo **1**:44–45
Arum **1**:46–47
Avocet **1**:50–51
Badger **1**:60–61
Bamboo **1**:62–63
Bass **2**:76–77
Bear **2**:82–85
Beaver **2**:86–87
Birch **2**:96–97
Bluebird **2**:110–111
Blue jay **2**:112–113
Bobcat **2**:114–115
Buffalo **2**:124–125
Cardinal **3**:148–149
Catfish **3**:154–155
Chickadee **3**:166–167
Chipmunk **3**:170–171
Cicada **3**:172–173
Club moss **3**:178–179
Condor **4**:202–203
Coot **4**:204–205
Crocodile **4**:226–227
Crow **4**:228–229
Cuckoo **4**:230–231
Deadly nightshade
    4:240–241
Deer **4**:242–245
Dormouse **5**:266–267
Dragonfly **5**:270–271
Earwig **5**:284–285
Eucalyptus **5**:302–303
Fig **5**:310–311
Firefly **5**:312–313
Flying squirrel **6**:332–333
Fox **6**:334–335
Foxglove **6**:336–337
Frog **6**:340–343
Gecko **6**:354–355
Ginkgo **6**:362–363
Goldfinch **6**:370–371

Grackle **6**:378–379
Grape **6**:380–381
Groundhog **7**:396–397
Hawk **7**:414–415
Hedgehog **7**:418–419
Hemlock **7**:420–421
Heron **7**:424–425
Holly **7**:430–431
Hornet **7**:436–437
Horsetail **7**:444–445
Hummingbird **7**:446–447
Kingfisher **8**:488–489
Kiwi **8**:490–491
Koala **8**:492–493
Kookaburra **8**:496–497
Lamprey **8**:504–505
Larch **8**:506–507
Leopard **9**:518–519
Lily **9**:522–523
Lime **9**:524–525
Limpkin **9**:526–527
Loon **9**:538–539
Magnolia **9**:546–547
Maple **9**:554–555
Merganser **9**:564–565
Mink **9**:570–571
Mistletoe **9**:572–573
Mockingbird **9**:574–575
Mole **10**:582–583
Muskrat **10**:608–609
Nightingale **10**:612–613
Nilgai **10**:616–617
Nuthatch **10**:620–621
Oak **10**:624–625
Oriole **11**:652–653
Osprey **11**:658–659
Otter **11**:662–663
Panda **11**:672–673
Perch **11**:688–689
Pine **11**:694–695
Pitcher plant **11**:702–703
Platypus **12**:710–711
Porcupine **12**:720–721
Puma **12**:740–741
Quail **12**:744–745
Quillwort **12**:748–749
Raccoon **12**:752–753
Robin **13**:784–785
Ruff **13**:790–791
Salamander **13**:794–795

Figures in **boldface type** indicate volume numbers

Salmon **13**:796–797
Sambar **13**:798–799
Sequoia **13**:816–817
Sesame **13**:818–819
Shrew **13**:826–827
Sparrow **14**:852–853
Sparrow hawk
  14:854–855
Squirrel **14**:868–869
Strawberry **14**:878–879
Sunflower **14**:888–889
Swan **14**:892–893
Tasmanian devil
  15:910–911

Tea **15**:912–913
Tiger **15**:928–929
Toad **15**:930–931
Trout **15**:940–941
Turkey **15**:946–947
Walking stick **16**:970–971
Wallaby **16**:972–973
Water lily **16**:980–981
Weasel **16**:984–985
Willow **16**:1006–1007
Wombat **16**:1010–1011

Woodpecker
  16:1014–1015

Tundra

Bear **2**:82–85
Bighorn sheep **2**:94–95
Caribou **3**:150–151
Coyote **4**:216–217
Fox **6**:334–335
Goat **6**:368–369

Figures in **boldface type** indicate volume numbers

Goose **6**:372–375
Hare **7**:412–413
Horsetail **7**:444–445
Lemming **8**:508–509
Loon **9**:538–539
Lynx **9**:542–543
Merganser **9**:564–565
Musk ox **10**:606–607
Polar bear **12**:714–715
Ptarmigan **12**:734–735
Ruff **13**:790–791
Shrew **13**:826–827
Weasel **16**:984–985
Yak **16**:1018–1019

Classification Index

ANIMALS

Amphibians and Reptiles

Amphibians
Axolotl **1**:52–53
Frog **6**:340–343
Salamander **13**:794–795
Toad **15**:930–931

Reptiles
Alligator **1**:26–27
Anaconda **1**:32–33
Chameleon **3**:160–161
Cobra **3**:180–181
Crocodile **4**:226–227
Gecko **6**:354–355
Gila monster **6**:360–361
Iguana **8**:464–465
Komodo dragon
   8:494–495
Monitor **10**:586–587
Python **12**:742–743
Rattlesnake **12**:762–763
Sidewinder **13**:830–831
Terrapin **15**:924–925
Tortoise **15**:934–935
Turtle **15**:948–951
Viper **15**:958–959
Water moccasin
   16:982–983

Birds

Albatross **1**:22–23
Avocet **1**:50–51
Bee-eater **2**:90–91
Bird of paradise **2**:98–99
Blackbird **2**:102–103
Bluebird **2**:110–111
Blue jay **2**:112–113
Bowerbird **2**:118–119
Bustard **2**:126–127
Cardinal **3**:148–149
Chickadee **3**:166–167
Cockatoo **3**:182–183

Condor **4**:202–203
Coot **4**:204–205
Crane **4**:220–221
Crow **4**:228–229
Cuckoo **4**:230–231
Curlew **4**:234–235
Dove **5**:268–269
Duck **5**:272–275
Eagle **5**:278–281
Emu **5**:300–301
Falcon **5**:304–305
Flamingo **5**:314–315
Frigate bird **6**:338–339
Gallinule **6**:350–351
Goldfinch **6**:370–371
Goose **6**:372–375
Grackle **6**:378–379
Grebe **7**:394–395
Grouse **7**:400–401
Gull **7**:404–405
Hawk **7**:414–415
Heron **7**:424–425
Honeyguide **7**:432–433
Hornbill **7**:434–435
Hummingbird **7**:446–447
Ibis **8**:462–463
Jacana **8**:470–471
Kestrel **8**:484–485
Killdeer **8**:486–487
Kingfisher **8**:488–489
Kiwi **8**:490–491
Kookaburra **8**:496–497
Limpkin **9**:526–527
Loon **9**:538–539
Macaw **9**:544–545
Merganser **9**:564–565
Mockingbird **9**:574–575
Nightingale **10**:612–613
Nuthatch **10**:620–621
Oriole **11**:652–653
Oropendola **11**:654–655
Osprey **11**:658–659
Ostrich **11**:660–661
Owl **11**:664–667

Oxpecker **11**:668–669
Parrot **11**:676–677
Peacock **11**:680–681
Pelican **11**:684–685
Penguin **11**:686–687
Petrel **11**:690–691
Pheasant **11**:692–693
Prairie chicken **12**:726–727
Ptarmigan **12**:734–735
Puffin **12**:738–739
Quail **12**:744–745
Quetzal **12**:746–747
Raven **12**:764–765
Rhea **13**:774–775
Roadrunner **13**:782–783
Robin **13**:784–785
Ruff **13**:790–791
Secretary bird **13**:814–815
Shoebill **13**:824–825
Skua **14**:840–841
Sparrow **14**:852–853
Sparrow hawk
   14:854–855
Starling **14**:872–873
Stork **14**:876–877
Sunbird **14**:886–887
Swallow **14**:890–891
Swan **14**:892–893
Swift **14**:894–895
Tern **15**:922–923
Toucan **15**:936–937
Turkey **15**:946–947
Vulture **16**:968–969
Weaver **16**:986–987
Woodpecker
   16:1014–1015

Fish

Angelfish **1**:34–35
Angler fish **1**:36–37
Barracuda **2**:74–75
Bass **2**:76–77
Carp **3**:152–153

Catfish **3**:154–155
Cod **3**:188–189
Coelacanth **3**:190–191
Eel **5**:288–289
Flying fish **6**:326–329
Grouper **7**:398–399
Halibut **7**:408–409
Herring **7**:426–427
Lamprey **8**:504–505
Lionfish **9**:530–531
Lungfish **9**:540–541
Marlin **9**:556–557
Mudskipper **10**:604–605
Ocean sunfish **10**:630–631
Perch **11**:688–689
Pipefish **11**:698–699
Piranha **11**:700–701
Puffer fish **12**:736–737
Ray **12**:766–767
Salmon **13**:796–797
Sea horse **13**:806–807
Shark **13**:820–823
Sturgeon **14**:880–881
Trout **15**:940–941
Tuna **15**:942–943
Wrasse **16**:1016–1017

Invertebrates

Ant **1**:38–39
Bee **2**:88–89
Beetle **2**:92–93
Black widow spider
   2:106–107
Butterfly **3**:134–137
Caddis fly **3**:140–141
Cicada **3**:172–173
Clam **3**:176–177
Cockroach **3**:184–185
Coral **4**:206–209
Crab **4**:218–219
Cranefly **4**:222–223
Cricket **4**:224–225
Dragonfly **5**:270–271
Earthworm **5**:282–283
Earwig **5**:284–285
Firefly **5**:312–313

Figures in **boldface type** indicate volume numbers

CLASSIFICATION INDEX

Flea **5**:316–317
Fly **5**:318–319
Grasshopper **7**:390–391
Hermit crab **7**:422–423
Hornet **7**:436–437
Horseshoe crab
  7:442–443
Hydra **8**:454–455
Jellyfish **8**:476–477
Ladybug **8**:498–499
Lobster **9**:536–537
Millipede **9**:566–567
Mosquito **10**:590–591
Moth **10**:594–597
Octopus **10**:634–635
Praying mantis
  12:730–731
Scorpion **13**:800–801
Sea anemone **13**:804–805
Sea urchin **13**:812–813
Shrimp **13**:828–829
Silkworm **14**:838–839
Slug **14**:846–847
Snail **14**:848–849
Spider **14**:856–859
Squid **14**:866–867
Starfish **14**:870–871
Tarantula **15**:908–909
Termite **15**:920–921
Walking stick **16**:970–971
Wasp **16**:978–979

Mammals

Aardvark **1**:14–15
African buffalo **1**:18–19
African wild dog **1**:20–21
Anteater **1**:40–41
Antelope **1**:42–43
Armadillo **1**:44–45
Baboon **1**:54–55
Badger **1**:60–61
Barbary ape **2**:72–73
Bat **2**:78–81
Bear **2**:82–85
Beaver **2**:86–87
Bighorn sheep **2**:94–95
Blackbuck **2**:104–105
Bobcat **2**:114–115
Buffalo **2**:124–125

Camel **3**:142–145
Capybara **3**:146–147
Caribou **3**:150–151
Chamois **3**:162–163
Cheetah **3**:164–165
Chimpanzee **3**:168–169
Chipmunk **3**:170–171
Colobus monkey
  4:200–201
Coyote **4**:216–217
Deer **4**:242–245
Dhole **4**:250–251
Dik-dik **4**:252–253
Dingo **4**:254–255
Dolphin **5**:262–263
Donkey **5**:264–265
Dormouse **5**:266–267
Dugong **5**:276–277
Echidna **5**:286–287
Eland **5**:290–291
Elephant **5**:292–295
Elephant shrew **5**:296–297
Elk **5**:298–299
Ferret **5**:308–309
Flying fox **6**:328–329
Flying lemur **6**:330–331
Flying squirrel **6**:332–333
Fox **6**:334–335
Galago **6**:348–349
Gazelle **6**:352–353
Gerbil **6**:356–357
Gibbon **6**:358–359
Giraffe **6**:364–365
Goat **6**:368–369
Gorilla **6**:376–377
Groundhog **7**:396–397
Guinea pig **7**:402–403
Gunn's bandicoot
  7:406–407
Hamster **7**:410–411
Hare **7**:412–413
Hedgehog **7**:418–419
Hippopotamus **7**:428–429
Horse **7**:438–441
Hyena **8**:456–457
Hyrax **8**:458–459
Ibex **8**:460–461

Impala **8**:466–467
Jackal **8**:472–473
Jaguar **8**:474–475
Kangaroo **8**:478–479
Kangaroo rat **8**:480–481
Koala **8**:492–493
Lemming **8**:508–509
Lemur **8**:510–511
Leopard **9**:518–519
Lion **9**:528–529
Llama **9**:534–535
Lynx **9**:542–543
Manatee **9**:548–549
Mandrill **9**:550–551
Marmoset **9**:558–559
Marsupial mole
  9:560–561
Meerkat **9**:562–563
Mink **9**:570–571
Mole **10**:582–583
Mongoose **10**:584–585
Moose **10**:588–589
Mouse **10**:600–603
Musk ox **10**:606–607
Muskrat **10**:608–609
Night monkey
  10:614–615
Nilgai **10**:616–617
Numbat **10**:618–619
Nutria **10**:622–623
Ocelot **10**:632–633
Okapi **10**:636–637
Opossum **11**:646–647
Orangutan **11**:648–649
Oryx **11**:656–657
Otter **11**:662–663
Panda **11**:672–673
Pangolin **11**:674–675
Peccary **11**:682–683
Pine marten
  11:696–697
Platypus **12**:710–711
Pocket gopher
  12:712–713
Polar bear **12**:714–715
Porcupine **12**:720–721
Porpoise **12**:722–723

Prairie dog **12**:728–729
Proboscis monkey
  12:732–733
Puma **12**:740–741
Rabbit **12**:750–751
Raccoon **12**:752–753
Rat **12**:760–761
Rhinoceros **13**:776–779
Saiga **13**:792–793
Sambar **13**:798–799
Seal **13**:808–809
Sea lion **13**:810–811
Shrew **13**:826–827
Skunk **14**:842–843
Sloth **14**:844–845
Springbok **14**:862–863
Squirrel **14**:868–869
Tamarin **15**:904–905
Tapir **15**:906–907
Tasmanian devil
  15:910–911
Tenrec **15**:918–919
Tiger **15**:928–929
Tree kangaroo
  15:938–939
Uakari **15**:952–953
Vole **16**:966–967
Wallaby **16**:972–973
Walrus **16**:974–975
Warthog **16**:976–977
Weasel **16**:984–985
Whale **16**:994–997
Wild cat **16**:1002–1003
Wildebeest
  16:1004–1005
Wolf **16**:1008–1011
Wombat **16**:1012–1013
Yak **16**:1018–1019
Zebra **16**:1022–1023

PLANTS

Cone-bearing plants

Bonsai **2**:112–113
Cycad **4**:236–237
Ginkgo **6**:362–363
Gnetophyte **6**:366–367
Larch **8**:506–507

Figures in **boldface type** indicate volume numbers

Pine **11**:694–695
Sequoia **13**:816–817
Weltwischia **16**:988–989

Flowering plants

Acacia **1**:16–17
Aloe **1**:28–29
Arum **1**:46–47
Avocado **1**:48–49
Bamboo **1**:62–63
Banksia **2**:70–71
Birch **2**:96–97
Bird-of-paradise flower
  2:100–101
Bladderwort **2**:108–109
Brazil nut tree **2**:120–121
Bromeliad **2**:122–123
Cactus **3**:138–139
Cattail **3**:156–157
Cinchona **3**:174–175
Coconut palm **3**:186–187
Coffee **4**:198–199
Corn **4**:212–213
Cotton **4**:214–215
Dandelion **4**:238–239
Deadly nightshade
  4:240–241
Eucalyptus **5**:302–303
Fig **5**:310–311
Foxglove **6**:336–337
Grape **6**:380–381
Grass **6**:382–383

Heather **7**:416–417
Hemlock **7**:420–421
Holly **7**:430–431
Lily **9**:522–523
Lime **9**:524–525
Magnolia **9**:546–547
Mangrove **9**:552–553
Maple **9**:554–555
Mimosa **9**:568–569
Mistletoe **9**:572–573
Mustard **10**:610–611
Oak **10**:624–625
Olive **10**:638–639
Orchid **11**:650–651
Palm **11**:670–671
Passionflower
  11:678–674
Pitcher plant **11**:702–703
Poppy **12**:718–719
Potato **12**:724–725
Rafflesia **12**:754–755
Rice **13**:780–781
Rose **13**:786–787
Rubber tree **13**:788–789
Sesame **13**:818–819
Soybean **14**:850–851
Spider plant **14**:860–861
Squash **14**:864–865
Stinging nettle
  14:874–875

Strawberry **14**:878–879
Sugarcane **14**:884–885
Sunflower **14**:888–889
Tea **15**:912–913
Tomato **15**:932–933
Venus flytrap **15**:956–957
Water lily **16**:980–981
Wheat **16**:998–999
Willow **16**:1006–1007
Yucca **16**:1020–1021

Seedless plants

Alga **1**:24–25
Club moss **3**:178–179
Fern **5**:306–307
Horsetail **7**:444–445
Kelp and other seaweeds
  8:482–483
Liverwort **9**:532–533
Moss **10**:592–593
Quillwort **12**:748–749
Whisk fern **16**:1000–1001

OTHER ORGANISMS

Alga **1**:24–25
Amoeba **1**:30–31
Bacterium **1**:56–59

Fungus **6**:344–347
Lichen **9**:520–521

BIOMES AND HABITATS

Cave **3**:158–159
Coral reef **4**:210–211
Cultivated land
  4:232–233
Desert **4**:246–249
Grassland **7**:392–393
Island **8**:468–469
Lake, river, and estuary
  8:500–503
Mountain **10**:598–599
Ocean **10**:626–629
Polar regions **12**:716
Rainforest **12**:756–759
Scrubland **13**:802–803
Suburban habitat
  14:882–883
Taiga **15**:902–903
Temperate forest
  15:914–917
Tide pool and coast
  15:926–927
Tundra **15**:944–945
Urban habitat **15**:954–955
Wetland **16**:990–993

Figures in **boldface type** indicate volume numbers

Scientific Names Index
Animals

A

Acanthaster planci (Crown-of-thorns starfish) **4**:209, 211

Accipiter gentilis (goshawk) **15**:903

Accipiter nisus (Sparrow hawk) **14:854–855**

Acinonyx jubatus (cheetah) **3**:164

Acipenser fulvescens (Lake sturgeon) **14**:880–881

Acipenser oxyrhynchus (Atlantic sturgeon) **14**:880, 881

Acipenser sturio (Atlantic sturgeon) **14**:880, 881

Acridotheres cristatellus (Crested myna) **14**:873

Acropora nobilis (Staghorn coral) **4**:207

Actias luna (Luna moth) **10**:596

Aepyceros melampus (impala) **8:466–467**

Agelaius phoeniceus (Red-winged blackbird) **2**:102, 103; **16**:991

Agkistrodon piscivorus (Water moccasin or cottonmouth) **16:982–983**, 993

Ailuropoda melanoleuca (Giant panda) **1**:63; **11:672–673**

Aix galericulata (Mandarin duck) **5**:272–273

Aix sponsa (American or Carolina wood duck) **5**:272, 274–275

Alcedo atthis (Common kingfisher) **8**:488

Alces alces (moose) **10:588–589**; **15**:903

Alicia mirabilis (Berried sea anemone) **13**:805

Alligator mississippiensis (American alligator) **1**:26, 27; **16**:993

Alopex lagopus (Arctic fox) **15**:945

Alytes obstetricans (Common midwife toad) **15**:931

Amazona viridigenalis (Red-crowned Amazon parrot) **11**:676

Amblyrhynchus cristatus (Marine iguana) **8**:464, 465

Ambystoma mexicanum (axolotl) **1:52–53**

Anax imperator (Emperor dragonfly) **5**:270, 271

Anax junius (North American dragonfly) **5**:270

Androctonus australis (Sanara scorpion) **13**:801

Anguilla anguilla (European eel) **5**:288–289

Anodorhynchus hyacinthinus (Hyacinth macaw) **9**:544

Anomalospiza imberbis (Cuckoo weaver) **16**:987

Anoura geoffroyi (Geoffroy's long-nosed bat) **2**:100

Anser caerulescens (Snow goose) **6**:372, 373, 374, 375

Antidorcas marsupialis (springbok) **14:862–863**

Antilocapra americana (pronghorn) **1:42–43**

Antilope cervicapra (blackbuck) **2:104–105**

Aotus trivirgatus (Night monkey) **10:614–615**

Aphonopelma chalcodes (Desert tarantula) **15**:908, 909

Apis mellifera (honeybee) **2**:88–89

Aptenodytes forsteri (Emperor penguin) **11**:686, 687

Aquila chrysaetos (Golden eagle) **5**:278, 279, 280, 281

Ara ararauna (Blue-and-yellow macaw) **9**:544

Ara chloropterus (Red-and-green macaw) **9**:544, 545

Aramus guarauna (limpkin) **9:526–527**

Archilochus colubris (Ruby-throated hummingbird) **7**:446, 447

Ardea cinerea (Gray heron) **16**:991

Ardea herodias (Great blue heron) **7**:424, 425

Ardeotis kori (Kori Bustard) **2**:127

Argiope trifasciata (Banded garden spider) **14**:856, 857

Arius felis (Sea catfish) **3**:155

Arothron meleagris (Spotted puffer fish) **12**:736, 737

Attacus atlas (Atlas moth) **10**:597

Aulacorhynchus huallagae (Yellow-browed toucanet) **15**:937

Azemiops feae (Fea's viper) **15**:959

B

Baillonius bailloni (Saffron toucanet) **15**:937

Balaeniceps rex (shoebill, Whale-headed stork or Shoe-billed stork) **13:824–825**

Balaenoptera musculus (Blue whale) **10**:628–629; **16**:994, 995, 996, 997

Barbus barbus (barbel) **8**:502

Bison bison (buffalo or bison) **2:124–125**

Bison bonasus (European bison) **2**:125

Bitis arietans (Puff adder) **15**:959

Bitis gabonica (Gaboon viper) **15**:958–959

Bitis peringuey (Peringuey's desert adder) **13**:831

Blastophaga psenes (Fig wasp) **5**:310–311

Bombyx mori (Chinese silkworm) **14**:838–839

Boselaphus tragocamelus (nilgai) **10:616–617**

Bos grunniens (yak) **16:1018–1019**

Brachypelma smithi (Mexican red knee) **15**:909

Bradypus tridactylus (Pale-throated three-toed sloth) **14**:844, 845

Branta canadensis (Canada goose) **6**:372, 374, 375

Bubo virginianus (Great horned owl) **4**:229; **11**:665, 667

Bufo americanus (American toad) **15**:930, 931

Bufo bufo (Common toad) **15**:90_

Bufo cognatus (Great plains toad) **15**:931

Bufo houstonensis (Houston toad) **15**:931

Bufo marinus (Giant marine toad) **15**:931

Buphagus erythrorhynchus (Yellow-billed oxpecker) **11**:668, 669

Buteo lineatus (Red-shouldered hawk) **7**:414, 415

C

Cacajao calvus (Bald, White, or Red uakari) **15**:952, 953

Cacajao melanocephalus (Black-headed uakari) **15**:952

Cacatua galerita (Sulfur-crested cockatoo) **3**:182, 183

Cacatua leadbeateri (Pink cockatoo) **3**:183

Calcarius lapponicus (Lapland bunting) **12**:716

Callithrix jacchus (Common marmoset) **9**:559

Camelus bactrianus (Bactrian camel) **3**:142; **4**:248

Camelus dromedarius (dromedary) **3**:142, 144–145; **4**:248

Campephilus imperialis (Imperial woodpecker) **16**:1015

Volume numbers are in **boldface type** followed by colons. Page numbers in **boldface type** indicate full articles.

ampephilus principalis (Ivory-billed woodpecker) **16**:1015

amposcia retusa (Decorator crab) **4**:218, 219

anis aureus (Golden jackal) **8**:472

anis familiaris dingo (dingo) **4:254–255**

anis latrans (coyote) **4:216–217**

anis lupus (Gray wolf) **15**:903, 945; **16**:1008, 1009, 1010

anis rufus (Red wolf) **16**:1010, 1011

apra ibex (ibex) **8:460–461**

archarodon carcharias (Great white shark) **4**:211; **13**:820, 821, 822

ardinalis cardinalis (Northern cardinal) **3**:148–149

arduelis hornemanni (Arctic redpoll) **12**:716

arduelis tristis (American goldfinch) **6**:370, 371

arollia perspicillata (Short-tailed leaf-nosed bat) **2**:78, 79

astor canadensis (Canadian beaver) **2**:86, 87

atagonus wagneri (Chacoan peccary) **11**:683

atharacta skua (Great skua) **14**:841

atharetes aura (Turkey buzzard) **16**:968, 969

avia porcellus (Domestic guinea pig) **7**:402, 403

ebuella pygmaea (Pygmy marmoset) **9**:558, 559

elastrina argiolus (Holly blue butterfly) **7**:431

entrocercus urophasianus (Sage grouse) **7**:400, 401

entruroides suffusus (Durango scorpion) **13**:801

ephalopholis miniata (Red grouper) **4**:211

eratotherium simum (White rhinoceros) **13**:776–777, 778, 779

ervus canadensis (elk or wapiti) **5:298–299**

Cervus elephus (Red deer) **5**:298

Cervus unicolor (sambar) **13:798–799**

Ceryle alcyon (Belted kingfisher) **8**:488, 489

Cetorhinus maximus (Basking shark) **13**:822

Chaetura pelagica (Chimney swift) **14**:894, 895

Chamaeleo chamaeleon (African or European chameleon) **3**:160

Charadrius vociferus (killdeer) **8:486–487**

Cheilinus undulatus (Humphead wrasse) **16**:1017

Chelydra serpentina (Snapping turtle) **8**:503

Chironectes minimus (Water opossum or yapok) **11**:646

Chironex fleckeri (Australian sea wasp) **8**:476

Chlamyphorus truncatus (Lesser or Pink, fairy armadillo) **1**:44

Choeropsis liberiensis (Pygmy hippopotamus) **7**:429

Chrysemys picta (Painted turtle) **15**:948, 949

Chrysolophus amherstiae (Lady Amherst's pheasant) **11**:692

Chrysolophus pictus (Golden pheasant) **11**:692

Ciconia ciconia (White stork) **14**:876

Circus cyaneus (Marsh hawk) **7**:414

Clarias batrachus (Walking catfish) **3**:155

Clupea harengus (herring) **7**:426

Coccinella septapunctata (Seven spot ladybug) **8**:499

Colinus virginianus (Bobwhite quail) **12**:744, 745

Collocalia fuciphaga (Edible-nest swiftlet) **14**:895

Colobus guereza (Black-and-white colobus monkey) **4**:200, 201

Columba livia (Rock dove) **5**:268, 269

Condylactus gigantea (Giant Caribbean sea anemone) **13**:804

Condylura cristata (Star-nosed mole) **10**:582, 583

Connochaetes gnou (Black wildebeest) **16**:1005

Connochaetes taurinus (Blue wildebeest) **16**:1004–1005

Conraua goliath (Goliath frog) **6**:340

Corvus brachyrhynchus (American crow) **4**:228

Corvus corax (Common or American raven) **12**:764, 765

Corvus cryptoleucus (Chihuahuan raven) **12**:764

Corvus fugilegus (rook) **4**:229

Coryphaeshna ingens (North American dragonfly) **5**:270

Cricetus cricetus (Common hamster) **7**:410–411

Crocodylus acutus (American crocodile) **4**:226, 227; **16**:993

Crocodylus porosus (Estuarine or Saltwater crocodile) **4**:226

Crocuta crocuta (Spotted hyena) **8**:457

Crotalus atrox (Western diamondback rattlesnake) **12**:762, 763

Crotalus cerastes (sidewinder) **13:830–831**

Cryptobranchus alleganiensis (hellbender) **13**:794, 795

Cuculus canorus (Common or European cuckoo) **4**:230, 231

Cuon alpinus (dhole) **4:250–251**

Cyanea capillata (North Atlantic giant violet jellyfish) **8**:477

Cyanocitta cristata (Blue jay) **2:112–113**

Cyanocitta stellari (Steller's jay) **2**:112

Cyanopsitta spixii (Spix's or Little blue macaw) **9**:545

Cygnus buccinator (Trumpeter swan) **14**:892

Cygnus columbianus columbianus (Whistling swan) **14**:892, 893

Cygnus olor (Mute swan) **14**:892

Cynocephalus variegatus (Malayan flying lemur) **6**:330, 331

Cynocephalus volans (Philippine flying lemur) **6**:330, 331

Cynomys ludovicianus (Black-tailed prairie dog) **12**:728

Cyprinus carpio (carp) **3**:153

D

Dacelo gigas (Laughing kookaburra) **8**:496, 497

Daktulosphai¯a vitifoliae (Grape phylloxera) **6**:381

Dama dama (Fallow deer) **4**:242, 243, 245

Danaus plexippus (Monarch butterfly) **3**:136, 137

Dasypus novemcinctus (Nine-banded armadillo) **1**:44–45

Deilephila elpenor (Elephant hawk moth) **10**:594

Delphinus delphis (Common dolphin) **5**:262; **16**:994

Dendrolagus inustus (Grizzled tree kangaroo) **15**:939

Dendrolagus lumholtzi (Lumholtz's tree kangaroo) **15**:938, 939

Dermochelys coriacea (Leatherback turtle) **15**:948, 950

Desmana moschata (Russian desman) **10**:583

Desmodus rotundus (Common vampire) **2**:79, 80, 81

Diceratias bispinosus (angler fish) **1**:37

Dicerorhinus sumatrensis (Sumatran rhinoceros) **13**:778

Diceros bicornis (Black rhinoceros) **13**:777–778, 779

Dicrostonyx groenlandicus (Collared lemming) **8**:508, 509

Didelphis virginiana (Common opossum) **15**:955

Volume numbers are in **boldface type** followed by colons. Page numbers in **boldface type** indicate full articles.

Didelphis virginiana (Common or Virginia opossum) **11**:646–647; **15**:955

Dinopis stauntoni (Net-throwing spider) **14**:858

Diomedea albatrus (Short-tailed albatross) **1**:23

Diomedea exulans (Wandering albatross) **1**:22, 23

Dipodomys merriami (Merriam's kangaroo rat) **8**:480, 481

Dromaius novaehollandiae (emu) **5:300–301**

Dryocopus pileatus (Pileated woodpecker) **16**:1014–1015

Dugong dugon (dugong) **5:276–277**

Dynastes hercules (Rhinoceros beetle) **2**:93

E

Echinops telfairi (Lesser hedgehog tenrec) **15**:918, 919

Echinothrix diadema (Diadem sea urchin) **13**:813

Echinus esculentus (Common sea urchin) **13**:812, 813

Echis carinatus (Saw-scaled viper) **15**:959

Electrophorus electricus (Electric eel) **5**:289

Elephantulus rozeti (North African elephant shrew) **5**:297

Elephantulus rufescens (Rufous elephant shrew) **5**:296, 297

Elephas maximus (Asian or Indian elephant) **5**:294, 295

Enhydra lutris (Sea otter) **11**:662–663

Ensifera ensifera (Andean sword-billed hummingbird) **7**:446–447

Eolophus roseicapillus (Galah or Rose-breasted cockatoo) **3**:183

Equus africanus (African donkey) **5**:264–265

Equus asinus (donkey or domestic ass) **5**:264

Equus burchelli (Common or Plains zebra) **16**:1022–1023

Equus caballus (Domestic horse) **7**:439

Equus grevyi (Grevy's zebra) **16**:1022, 1023

Equus przewalski (Przewalski's horse) **7**:440, 441

Equus zebra (Mountain zebra) **16**:1022–1023

Erethizon dorsatum (North American porcupine) **12**:721

Erinaceus europaeus (Western European hedgehog) **7**:418, 419

Eristicophis macmahoni (McMahon's viper) **13**:831

Erithacus rubecula (European robin) **13**:784, 785

Esox lucius (Northern pike) **8**:501–502

Eudocimus albus (White ibis) **8**:462, 463

Eunectes murinus (Green anaconda) **1**:32, 33

Eunectes notaeus (Southern anaconda) **1**:32

Euphractus sexcinetus (Six-banded armadillo) **1**:44

Eutamias sibiricus (Asiatic or Siberian chipmunk) **3**:171

Exocoetus volitans (Flying fish) **6**:327

F

Falco peregrinus (Peregrine falcon) **5**:304, 305; **15**:954–955

Falco rusticolus (Gyr falcon) **5**:304

Falco sparverius (American kestrel) **8**:484, 485; **14**:855

Felis caracal (caracal) **9**:543

Felis concolor coryi (Florida panther) **16**:993

Felis concolor (puma, cougar, or Mountain lion) **12:740–741**

Felis lynx (lynx) **9**:519, **542–543**; **15**:903

Felis pardalis (ocelot) **10:632–633**

Felis rufus (bobcat) **2:114–115**; **9**:519

Felis silvestris (Wild cat) **16:1002–1003**

Felis wiedii (Margay cat) **10**:632

Fennecus zerda (Fennec fox) **4**:248

Forficula auricularia (Common earwig) **5**:284, 285

Fratercula arctica (Atlantic or Common puffin) **12**:738, 739

Fregata andrewsi (Andrew's frigate bird) **6**:339

Fregata magnificens (Magnificent frigate bird) **6**:338, 339

Fulica americana (American coot) **4**:204–205

G

Gadus morhua (Atlantic cod) **3**:188

Galemys pyrenaicus (Pyrenean desman) **10**:583

Gallinula chloropus (Common moorhen) **6**:351

Garrulus glandarius (Common or European jay) **2**:113

Gavia immer (Common loon or Great northern diver) **9**:539

Gazella thomsoni (Thomson's gazelle) **6**:352, 353

Gecarcoidea natalis (Red land crab) **4**:218, 219

Geococcyx californianus (Greater roadrunner) **13**:782, 783

Geococcyx velox (Lesser roadrunner) **13**:783

Giraffa camelopardalis (giraffe) **6:364–365**

Glaucomys sabrinus (Northern flying squirrel) **6**:332

Glaucomys volans (Northern flying squirrel) **15**:903

Glirulus japonicus (Japanese dormouse) **5**:267

Glis glis (Fat or Edible dormouse) **5**:266–267

Gopherus polyphemus (Gopher tortoise) **15**:934, 935

Gorilla gorilla (gorilla) **6:376–37**

Gracula religiosa (Hill myna) **14**:873

Graphiurus murinus (African dormouse) **5**:267

Graptemys geographica (Geographi or Map terrapin) **15**:924

Grus canadensis (Sandhill crane) **4**:220, 221

Gulo gulo (wolverine) **15**:945

Gygis alba (White tern) **15**:923

Gymnothorax flavimarginatus (Leopard moray eel) **4**:211; **5**:288, 289

H

Hadrurus arizonensis (Giant desert hairy scorpion) **13**:800, 801

Haliaeetus leucocephalus (Bald eagle) **5**:278, 279; **16**:993

Halichoeres bivittatus (Slippery Dick wrasse) **16**:1017

Hapalochlaena maculosa (Blue-ringed octopus) **10**:634, 635

Heliothis armegera (American bollworm) **4**:215

Heliothis zea (Corn earworm) **4**:215

Heloderma suspectum (Gila monster) **6:360–361**

Helogale parvula (Dwarf mongoose) **10**:585

Henricia leviscula (Blood star) **14**:870, 871

Herpestes edwardsi (Indian gray mongoose) **10**:584–585

Herpestes ichneumon (Egyptian mongoose) **10**:585

Himantolophus groenlandicus (Football fish) **1**:37

Hippocampus ingens (Pacific sea horse) **13**:806

Hippocampus zosterae (Dwarf sea horse) **13**:806, 807

Hippoglossus hippoglossus (Atlantic halibut) **7**:408

Hippopotamus amphibius (hippopotamus) **7:428–429**

Volume numbers are in **boldface type** followed by colons.
Page numbers in **boldface type** indicate full articles.

rundo rustica (Barn swallow)
14:890, 891

marus americanus (American
lobster) **9**:536, 537

so huso (beluga) **14**:881

alophora cecropia (Robin moth)
10:597

drochoerus hydrochaeris
(capybara) **3:146–147**

drodamalis gigas (Steller's sea
cow) **9**:548

la crucifer (Spring peeper)
16:992

lobates syndactylus (Siamang
gibbon) **6**:359

K

alurus nebulosus (Brown
bullhead) **3**:155

erus galbula (Northern oriole)
11:652–653

dicator indicator (Greater
honeyguide) **1**:61; **7:432–433**

dicator variegatus (Scaly-throated
honeyguide) **7**:433

rus oxyrinchus (Shortfin mako)
13:821

cana spinosa (Northern or
American jacana) **8**:470, 471

tsuwonus pelamis (Skipjack tuna
or bonito) **15**:942–943

broides dimidiatus (Cleaner
wrasse) **4**:211; **16**:1016, 1017

gopus lagopus (Willow grouse)
12:734, 735; **15**:945

gopus mutus (ptarmigan)
12:734–735; 15:945

gopus scoticus (Red grouse)
7:417

ma glama (llama) **9:534–535**

rus argentatus (Herring gull)
7:404–405

timeria chalumnae (coelacanth)
3:190–191

trodectus sp. (Black widow
spider) **2:106–107; 14**:858

mmus lemmus (Norway
lemming) **8**:508, 509

Lemur catta (Ring-tailed lemur)
8:510, 511

Leontopithecus rosalia (Golden lion
tamarin) **15**:904, 905

Lepomis gibbosas (sunfish) **8**:503

Leptonycteris curasoae (Lesser long-
nosed bat) **3**:139

Leptoptilos crumeniferus (marabou)
14:877

Lepus californicus (Black-tailed
jackrabbit) **12**:750, 751

Lepus timidus (Arctic hare)
7:412–413; **15**:945

Liberiictis kuhni (Liberian
mongoose) **10**:585

Litocranius walleri (East African
giraffe antelope) **6**:352

Locustana pardalina (Brown
locust) **7**:391

Loligo pealii (Longfin squid)
14:866

Lophius americanus (goosefish) **1**:36

Lophius piscatorius (angler fish)
1:36

Lophodytes cucullatus (Hooded
merganser) **9**:564, 565

Loxocemus bicolor (Mexican
burrowing python) **12**:742

Loxodonta africana (African
elephant) **5**:292, 293, 294

Loxosceles reclusa (Brown recluse
spider) **14**:858

Lucanus cervus (Stag beetle) **2**:93

Lumbricus terrestris (Common
earthworm) **5**:282

Luscinia megarhynchos (Common
nightingale) **10**:612–613

Lutra canadensis (North American
river otter) **11**:662

Lycaon pictus (African wild dog
or Cape hunting dog)
1:20–21

Lycosa tarantula (a tarantula)
15:908

Lytocarpia nuttingi (an hydrozoan)
8:455

M

Macaca silenus (Lion-tailed
macaque) **2**:72

Macaca sylvanus (Barbary ape)
2:72–73

Macropus agilis (Agile wallaby)
16:972, 973

Macropus dorsalis (Black-striped
wallaby) **16**:973

Macropus parma (Parma wallaby)
16:973

Macropus rufus (Red kangaroo)
8:478–479

Madoqua kirki (Kirk's dik-dik)
4:252, 253

Makaira indica (Black marlin)
9:556, 557

Makaira nigricans (Blue marlin)
9:557

Malaclemys terrapin (Diamond-back
terrapin) **15**:924–925; **16**:991

Mandrillus sphinx (mandrill)
9:550–551

Manduca sexta (Tobacco hawk
moth) **4**:233; **10**:594–596

Manis temmincki (Cape pangolin)
11:674, 675

Manta birostris (Atlantic manta
ray or devilray) **12**:766, 767

Marmota monax (groundhog or
woodchuck) **7:396–397**

Martes americana (American pine
marten) **11**:696, 697

Martes zibellina (sable) **15**:903

Megaptera novaeangliae (Humpback
whale) **16**:994, 995–996

Melanocetus johnsonii (Football
fish) **1**:37

Melanosuchus niger (Black cayman)
1:27

Meleagris gallopavo (Wild turkey)
15:946, 947

Mellisuga helenae (Cuban bee
hummingbird) **7**:446

Mellita quinquiesperforata (Keyhole
urchin) **13**:813

Mellivora capensis (Honey badger)
1:60, 61

Mephitis macroura (Hooded skunk)
14:842

Mephitis mephitis (Striped or
Common skunk)
14:842–843

Mergus merganser (Common
merganser) **9**:564, 565

Mergus serrator (Red-breasted
merganser) **9**:564, 565

Mergus squamatus (Scaly-sided
merganser) **9**:565

Meriones unguiculatus (Mongolian
gerbil) **6**:356, 357

Merops apiaster (European bee-
eater) **2**:91

Merops nubicus (Carmine bee-
eater) **2**:91

Mesocricetus auratus (Golden
hamster) **7**:410, 411

Microbuthus pusillus (Middle
Eastern scorpion) **13**:800

Micromys minutus (Harvest mouse)
4:233

Micropsitta pusio (New Guinean
buff-faced pygmy parrot)
11:677

Micropterus salmoides (Largemouth
bass) **2**:76–77

Microsorex hayi (Pygmy shrew)
13:827

Microtus agrestis (Field vole)
16:966, 967

Mimus polyglottos (Northern
mockingbird) **9**:574, 575

Mirounga angustirostris (Northern
elephant seal) **13**:808, 809

Mola mola (Ocean sunfish or
trunkfish) **10:630–631**

Monodon monoceros (narwhal)
16:994

Mungos mungo (Banded
mongoose) **10**:585

Muscardinus avellanarius
(dormouse) **15**:917

Mus musculus (House mouse)
10:600–601

Mustela lutreola (European mink)
9:571

Volume numbers are in **boldface type** followed by colons.
Page numbers in **boldface type** indicate full articles.

Mustela nigripes (Black-footed ferret) **5**:308–309

Mustela nivalis (Least weasel) **16**:984–985

Mustela vison (American mink) **9**:570, 571; **15**:903

Mycteria americana (Wood stork) **14**:876–877; **16**:992

Myctophum punctatum (lanternfish) **10**:629

Myocastor coypus (nutria) **10:622–623**

Myrmecophaga tridactyla (Giant anteater) **1:40–41**

N

Naja haje (Egyptian cobra) **3**:180, 181

Nasalis larvatus (Proboscis monkey) **12:732–733**

Nectarinia famosa (Malacite sunbird) **14**:887

Nectarinia jugularis (Yellow-bellied sunbird) **14**:886

Nectophrynoides occidentalis (West African live-bearing toad) **15**:931

Negaprion brevirostris (Lemon shark) **13**:822

Neobatrachus pictus (Meeoioing frog) **6**:341

Neoceratodus forsteri (Australian lungfish) **9**:540, 541

Neofelis nebulosa (Clouded leopard) **9**:519

Neophocaena phocaenoides (Finless porpoise) **12**:722

Neophron pernopterus (Egyptian vulture) **16**:969

Notoryctes typhlops (Marsupial mole) **9:560–561**

Numenius americanus (Long-billed curlew) **4**:234–235

Nymphicus hollandicus (Gray cockatiel) **3**:182

O

Oceanites oceanicus (Wilson's storm petrel) **11**:690, 691

Octopus vulgaris (Common octopus) **10**:634–635

Odobenus rosmarus (walrus) **16:974–975**

Odocoileus virginianus (White-tailed deer) **4**:242, 244, 245

Oecanthus fultoni (Tree cricket) **4**:225

Okapi johnstoni (okapi) **10:636–637**

Ondatra zibethicus (muskrat) **10:608–609**

Onychogalea fraenata (Brindled nailtail wallaby) **16**:972–973

Onymacris unguicularis (Tenebrionid beetle) **4**:249

Orcinus orca (Killer whale or orca) **5**:263; **16**:996, 997

Oreamnos americanus (North American mountain goat) **6**:368, 369

Orectolobus ornatus (Ornate wobbegong) **13**:822

Ornithorhynchus anatinus (Duck-billed platypus) **12:710–711**

Orycteropus afer (aardvark) **1:14–15**

Oryx gazella (African oryx) **11**:656, 657

Otis gurneyi (Giant scops owl) **11**:667

Otus rutilus capnodes (Anjouan scops owl) **11**:667

Ovibos moschatus (Musk ox) **10:606–607; 15**:945

Ovis canadensis (Bighorn sheep) **2:94–95; 10**:599

P

Pandion haliaetus (osprey) **11:658–659**

Pan paniscus (Pygmy chimpanzee or bonobo) **3**:169

Panthera leo (lion) **9:528–529**

Panthera onca (jaguar) **8:474–475**

Panthera pardus (leopard) **9:518–519**

Panthera tigris (tiger) **15:928–929**

Panthera tigris sumatrae (Sumatran tiger) **15**:928

Panthera uncia (Snow leopard or ounce) **9**:519; **10**:599

Pan troglodytes (Common chimpanzee) **3**:169

Papio hamadryas (Hamadryas or Sacred baboon) **1**:54, 55

Papio hamadryas cycnocephalus (Common baboon) **1**:54

Papio hamadryas papio (Guinea baboon) **1**:54

Paracheirodon innesi (Neon tetra) **11**:701

Paradisea gulielmi (Emperor of Germany's bird of paradise) **2**:99

Parus atricapillus (Black-capped chickadee) **3**:166, 167

Passer domesticus (House sparrow) **14:852–853**

Pavo cristatus (Indian peacock) **11**:680, 681

Pectinophora gossypiella (Pink bollworm) **4**:215

Pelecanus erythrorhynchos (American white pelican) **11:684–685**

Perameles gunnii (Gunn's bandicoot) **7:406–407**

Perca flavescens (American perch) **11**:688, 689

Perca fluviatilis (European perch) **11**:688, 689

Periplaneta americana (American cockroach) **3**:185; **15**:955

Peromyscus leucopus (White-footed mouse) **10**:601

Peromyscus maniculatus (Deer mouse) **10**:602

Petromyzon marinus (Sea lamprey) **8**:504, 505

Phacochoerus aethiopicus (warthog) **16:976–977**

Pharomachru mocino (Resplendent quetzal) **12**:746, 747

Phascolarctos cinereus (koala) **5**:302; **8:492–493**

Phasianus colchicus (Common pheasant) **11**:692, 693

Philetarius socius (Sociable weaver) **16**:986

Philomachus pugnax (ruff) **13:790–791**

Phocoena phocoena (Harbor porpoise) **12**:722, 723

Phocoena sinus (Gulf of California porpoise) **12**:723

Phocoena spinipinnis (Burmeister's porpoise) **12**:723

Phocoenoides dalli (Dall's porpoise) **12**:722; **16**:994

Phoenicopterus ruber (Greater flamingo) **5**:314, 315

Photuris pennsylvanicus (Eastern firefly) **5**:312

Phrynosoma cornutum (Texas horned lizard) **8**:465

Phyllopteryx taeniolatus (Weedy seadragon) **13**:806

Physeter catodon (Sperm whale) **16**:994, 995, 996

Pipa pipa (Surinam toad) **15**:931

Plecotus auritus (Brown long-eared bat) **2**:81

Ploceus philippinus (Baya weaverbird) **16**:986

Ploceus velatus (Southern masked weaver) **16**:987

Podiceps grisegena (Red-necked grebe) **7**:394, 395

Pomacanthus imperator (Emperor angelfish) **1:34–35**

Pomacanthus semicirculatus (Blue angelfish) **1**:35

Pomacea caliginosa (a snail) **9**:526

Pongo pygmaeus (orangutan) **11:648–649**

Porphyrio martinicus (Purple gallinule) **6**:351

Priodontes maximus (Giant armadillo) **1**:44

Pristophora erichsonii (Larch sawfly) **8**:507

Prosciger aterrimus (Great black or Palm cockatoo) **3**:182

Volume numbers are in **boldface type** followed by colons.
Page numbers in **boldface type** indicate full articles.

rocavia capensis (Cape rock hyrax) **8**:458

rocolobus badius (Guinea Forest red colobus monkey) **4**:200

rocolobus pennantii (Pennant's red colobus) **4**:201

rocolobus verus (Olive colobus) **4**:201

rocyon lotor (North American raccoon) **12**:752, 753; **15**:955

rogne subis (Purple martin) **15**:954–955

roteus anguinus (manfish) **3**:158, 159

rotopterus aethiopicus (African lungfish) **9**:540–541

arocolius decumanus (Crested oropendola) **11**:654, 655

ephotus chrysopterygius (Golden-shouldered parrot) **11**:677

eudomyrmex ferruginea (Acacia ant) **1**:16, 17

eudotriton ruber ruber (Northern red salamander) **13**:794

erocnemia pennata (Darwin's rhea) **13**:775

eronura brasiliensis (Giant otter) **11**:662

eropus giganteus (Indian flying fox) **6**:328, 329

ilonorhynchus violaceus (Satin bowerbird) **2**:118, 119

cnopodia helianthoides (Many-rayed star) **14**:870

gocentrus piraya (a piranha) **11**:700, 701

thon reticulatus (Reticulated python) **12**:742, 743

thon sebae (African rock python) **12**:742

R

iiscalus quiscula (Common grackle) **6**:378, 379

mphastos toco (Toco toucan) **15**:936, 937

na catesbeiana (American bullfrog) **6**:340, 341

ngifer tarandus (caribou) **3**:150–151; **15**:945

Raphus cucullatus (dodo) **8**:469

Rattus norvegicus (Brown rat) **12**:760, 761; **15**:954

Recurvirostra americana (American avocet) **1**:50–51

Recurvirostra avosetta (Eurasian avocet) **1**:51

Recurvirostra novaehollandiae (Red-necked avocet) **1**:51

Rhea americana (Common rhea) **13**:774, 775

Rhincodon typus (Whale shark) **13**:821, 822, 823

Rhinoceros sondaicus (Javan rhinoceros) **13**:778

Rhinoceros unicornis (Indian rhinoceros) **13**:776, 778

Rhinophrynus dorsalis (Burrowing toad) **15**:931

Rhombomys opimus (Giant or Great gerbil) **6**:356, 357

Rooseveltiella nattereri (Natterer's or Red piranha) **11**:700

Rupicapra rupicapra (chamois) **3:162–163**; **10**:599

S

Sagittarius serpentarius (Secretary bird) **13:814–815**

Saguinus oedipus (Cotton-top tamarin) **15**:905

Saiga tatarica (saiga) **13:792–793**

Salmo gairdneri (Rainbow trout) **15**:940–941

Salmo salar (Atlantic salmon) **13**:796, 797

Salmo trutta (Brown trout) **15**:941

Sarcophilus harrisii (Tasmanian devil) **15:910–911**

Scalopus aquaticus (Eastern mole) **10**:582

Scaphyrinchus platorynchus (Shovelnose sturgeon) **14**:881

Sceloporus undulatus (Eastern fence lizard) **8**:465

Schistocera gregaria (Desert locust) **7**:391

Sciurus carolinensis (Eastern gray squirrel) **14**:868, 869; **15**:955

Scorpaensis scrofa (scorpion fish) **4**:211

Selevinia betpakdalaensis (Desert dormouse) **5**:267

Setifer setosus (Greater hedgehog tenrec) **15**:918

Sialia sialis (Eastern bluebird) **2**:111; **14**:873

Sitta carolinensis (White-breasted nuthatch) **10**:620, 621

Somateria mollissima (Common eider duck) **5**:275

Souromalus obesus (Chuckwalla) **8**:465

Sphyma zygaena (Common hammerhead) **13**:821

Sphyraena barracuda (Great barracuda) **2**:74, 75

Stereolepis gigas (Giant sea bass) **2**:77

Sterna fuscata (Sooty tern) **15**:922

Sterna paradisaea (Arctic tern) **15**:922, 923, 945

Streptoprocne zonaris (White-collared swift) **14**:895

Strigops habroptilus (kakapo) **8**:469

Strix nebulosa (Great gray owl) **11**:664–665, 666

Strix occidentalis (Spotted owl) **11**:667

Struthio camelus (ostrich) **7**:393; **11:660–661**

Sturnus vulgaris (Common starling) **14**:872, 873

Suricata suricatta (meerkat or suricate) **9:562–563**; **10**:585

Synceros caffer (African buffalo) **1:18–19**

Syngnathus acus (Great pipefish) **11**:698–699

Syngnathus californiensis (Kelp pipefish) **11**:699

T

Tachyglossus aculeatus (Spiny anteater) **5**:286, 287

Tamias minimus (Least chipmunk) **3**:171

Tamias striatus (Eastern chipmunk) **3**:170

Tapirus bairdii (Baird's tapir) **15**:906

Tapirus indicus (Malayan tapir) **15**:906

Tapirus pinchaque (Mountain tapir) **15**:906

Tapirus terrestris (South American or Brazilian tapir) **15**:906, 907

Taurotragus derbianus (Giant eland) **5**:291

Taurotragus oryx (eland) **5:290–291**

Taxidea taxus (American badger) **1:60–61**

Tayassu pecari (White-lipped peccary) **11**:683

Tayassu tajacu (Collared peccary) **11**:682–683

Tenodera aridifolia (Chinese praying mantis) **12**:731

Tenrec ecaudatus (Common or Tailless tenrec) **15**:918–919

Testudo elephantopus (Giant tortoise) **15**:935

Tetrao urogallus (capercaillie) **15**:903

Tetrapturus albidus (White marlin) **9**:557

Tetrapturus audax (Striped marlin) **9**:557

Tettigonia viridissima (Great green bush cricket) **4**:224

Theraphosa leblondi (Goliath bird-eating spider) **15**:909

Thomomys bottae (Botta's pocket gopher) **12**:713

Threskiornis aethiopicus (Sacred ibis) **8**:462

Thunnus albacares (Yellowfin tuna) **15**:943

Thunnus thynnus (Bluefin tuna or tunny) **10**:629; **15**:942, 943

Tockus erythrorhynchus (Red-billed hornbill) **7**:434, 435

Volume numbers are in **boldface type** followed by colons. Page numbers in **boldface type** indicate full articles.

Torpedo nobiliana (Atlantic torpedo ray) **12**:767

Tremarctos ornatus (Spectacled bear) **2**:82, 85

Trichechus manatus (West Indian manatee) **9**:548, 549

Turdus migratorius (American robin) **13**:784–785

Tursiops truncatus (Bottlenose dolphin) **5**:262, 263

Tympanuchus cupido (Greater prairie chicken) **12**:726–727

Tyto alba (Barn owl) **11**:664, 665

UV

Ursus americanus (Black bear) **15**:903

Ursus arctos horribilis (Grizzly bear) **2**:82, 83–84

Ursus maritimus (Polar bear) **12:714–715**

Ursus ursus (Brown bear) **15**:903

Varanus gouldii (Gould's or Sand monitor) **10**:586, 587

Varanus komodoensis (Komodo dragon) **8**:469, **494–495**

Vipera berus (adder) **15**:903

Vombatus ursinus (Common or Coarse-haired wombat) **16**:1013

Vulpes macrotis (Desert sand fox) **4**:249

Vulpes vulpes (Red fox) **6**:334–335; **15**:955

Vultus gryphus (Andean condor) **4**:202–203

WXY

Wallabia bicolor (Swamp wallaby) **16**:972, 973

Xenicus lyalli (Flightless wren) **8**:469

Xenopsylla cheopis (Tropical rat flea) **5**:317

Z

Zaglossus bruijni (Long-nosed echidna) **5**:287

Zalophus californianus (California sea lion) **13**:810–811

Zapus hudsonius (Meadow jumping mouse) **10**:602, 603

Zenkerella insignis (Flightless scaly tailed squirrel) **6**:333

Plants

A

Acacia cornigera (Bull's horn acacia) **1**:16–17

Acacia senegal (Senegal acacia) **1**:17

Acer platanoides (Norway maple) **9**:554

Acer rubrum (Red maple) **9**:554, 555; **16**:992

Acer saccharinum (Silver maple) **9**:555

Acer saccharum (Sugar maple) **9**:554, 555

Acer sempervirens (Cretan maple) **9**:554

Aldrovanda vesiculosa (Waterwheel plant) **15**:957

Allium cepa (onion) **9**:523

Allium sativum (garlic) **9**:523

Aloe vera (true aloe) **1:28–29**

Ananas comosus (pineapple) **2**:122, 123

Anemone coronaria (Lily of the field) **9**:523

Anthriscus sylvestris (Cow parsley) **7**:421

Arenga pinnata (Asian sugar palm) **11**:671

Argemone mexicana (Mexican poppy) **12**:719

Arisaema triphyllum (jack-in-the-pulpit) **1**:46–47

Asparagus officinalis (asparagus) **9**:523

Asplenium bulbiferum (Mother spleenwort) **5**:307

Asplenium nidus (Bird's nest fern) **5**:307

Aster mohavensis (Desert aster) **4**:247

Atriplex hymenelytra (Desert holly) **4**:249

Atropa belladonna (Deadly nightshade) **4:240–241**

B

Bambusa vulgaris (Common bamboo) **1**:62–63

Banksia grandis (Bull banksia) **2**:70

Banksia serrata (Red honeysuckle) **2**:71

Bertholletia excelsa (Brazil nut tree) **2:120–121**

Betula papyrifer (Paper birch) **15**:916

Boehmeria nivea (China grass) **14**:874

Brassica juncea (Asian brown mustard) **10**:611

Brassica nigra (Black mustard) **10**:611

C

Calluna vulgaris (heather; Scotch heather; ling) **7**:416, 417

Camellia sinensis (tea plant) **15:712–713**

Camellia sinensis var. *assamica* (Assam tea) **15**:712, 713

Camptosorus rhizophyllus (Walking fern) **5**:307

Carnegiea gigantea (Saguaro cactus) **3**:138, 139

Caryota urens (Toddy palm) **11**:671

Cecropia **14**:844

Cephalotus follicularis (Albany pitcher plant) **11**:702

Chlorophytum comosum (spider plant) **14:860–861**

Chondrus crispus (Irish moss) **15**:926

Chrysanthemum segetum (Corn marigold) **4**:233

Cibotium barometz (a fern) **5**:307

Cinchona spp. (cinchona) **3:174–175**

Citrus aurantifolia (lime tree) **9**:524, 525

Cocos nucifera (Coconut palm) **3:186–187; 11**:671

Coffea arabica (Arabian coffee) **4**:198–199

Coffea canephora (Congo coffee) **4**:198, 199

Coffea liberica (Liberian coffee) **4**:198

Conium maculatum (Poison hemlock) **7:420–421**

Convallaria majalis (Lily of the valley) **9**:523

Cortaderia selloana (Pampas grass) **6**:382, 383

Couroupita guianensis (Cannonball tree) **2**:120, 121

Cryptothallus mirabilis (a liverwort) **9**:533

Cucurbita pepo (a squash) **14**:864

Cycas revoluta (sago palm) **4**:236, 237

D

Darlingtonia californica (California pitcher plant or Cobra lily) **11:702–703**

Datura stramonium (jimsonweed or Thorn apple) **4**:241

Digitalis lanata (Woolly or Austrian foxglove) **6**:337

Digitalis purpurea (Common or Purple foxglove) **6**:336–337

Dionaea muscipula (Venus flytrap) **15:956–957; 16**:991

Dioon edule (a cycad) **4**:237

Volume numbers are in **boldface type** followed by colons. Page numbers in **boldface type** indicate full articles.

F

chinocactus ingens (a cactus) **3**:138

mbothrium coccineum (Chilean fire bush) **2**:70

ncephalartos transvenosus (a cycad) **4**:237

schscholzia californica (Californian poppy) **12**:718, 719

ucalyptus diversicolor (karri) **5**:302

ucalyptus leucoxylon (ironbark) **5**:302

ucalyptus niphophila (Snow gum) **5**:302

ucalyptus regnans (Giant gum tree or Mountain ash) **5**:302

icus aura (Strangler fig) **5**:310, 311

icus benghalensis (East Indian fig or Banyan tree) **5**:311

icus carica (Common fig) **5**:311

ragaria ananassa (Cultivated strawberry) **14**:879

ragaria chiloensis (Chile strawberry) **14**:878

ragaria virginiana (a strawberry) **14**:878

ucus sargassum (rockweed) **15**:926

G

alium aparine (goosegrass) **3**:175

ardenia jasminoides (Cape jasmine) **3**:175

inkgo biloba (ginkgo or Maidenhair tree) **6:362–363**

lycine max (soya plant) **14:850–851**

netum gnemon (a gnetophyte) **6**:366, 367

netum leptostachyum (a gnetophyte) **6**:367

ossypium barbadense (cotton) **4**:214, 215

ossypium hirsutum (cotton) **4**:214

I–K

elianthus annuus (sunflower) **4**:239; **14:888–889**

emileia vastatrix (coffee leaf rust) **4**:199

Hevea brasiliensis (Brazilian rubber tree) **13:788–789**

Hordeum vulgare (barley) **6**:382

Hyoscyamus niger (henbane) **4**:241

Ilex aquifolium (English holly) **7**:430, 431

Ilex guianensis (a holly) **7**:430–431

Ilex opaca (American holly) **7**:430, 431

Ilex paraguariensis (Yerba maté) **7**:431

Isoetes histrix (a quillwort) **12**:748

Isoetes lacustris (a quillwort) **12**:749

Isoetes louisianensis (Louisiana quillwort) **12**:748, 749

Isoetes melanospora (Black-spored quillwort) **12**:749

Isoetes tegetiformans (Mat-forming quillwort) **12**:749

L

Lagenaria cylindrica (a gourd) **14**:864

Lagenaria siceraria (Bottle gourd) **14**:864

Laminaria digitata (kelp) **8**:482–483

Laminaria hyperborea (a kelp) **10**:626

Lappula sharsmithii (Alpine forget-me-not) **10**:598

Larix dahurica (Dahurian larch) **15**:902–903

Larix decidua (European larch) **8**:506–507

Larix griffithiana (Sikkim larch) **8**:506

Larix kaempferi (Japanese larch) **8**:507

Larix laricina (Eastern larch) **8**:507

Larix occidentalis (Western larch) **8**:506, 507

Lecythis zabucajo **2**:120

Lepidozamia hopei (a cycad) **4**:237

Lepidozamia peroffskyana (a cycad) **4**:237

Leptospermum scorparium (tea-tree) **5**:303

Lilium bulbiferum (Bulb-bearing lily) **9**:523

Lilium candidum (Madonna lily) **9**:523

Lilium superbum (Turk's cap lily) **9**:522, 523

Lycopodium clavatum (Stag's horn moss) **3**:178

Lycopodium obscurum (ground pine) **3**:178, 179

Lysichitum americianum (Yellow skunk cabbage) **1**:47

Lythrum salicaria (Purple loosestrife) **3**:157

M

Macadamia integrifolia (Macadamia nut) **2**:70

Macrocystis pyrifera (Giant kelp) **8**:482, 483; **10**:628

Magnolia acuminata (Cucumber tree) **9**:547

Magnolia grandiflora (Bull bay or Southern magnolia) **9**:546, 547

Magnolia tripetala (Umbrella tree) **9**:547

Magnolia virginiana (Sweet bay magnolia) **9**:547

Marchantia polymorpha (a liverwort) **9**:532, 533

Matteuccia struthiopteris (Ostrich fern) **5**:307

Meconopsis betonicifolia (Himalayan poppy) **12**:718

Melaleuca leucadendron **5**:303

Metzgeria furcata (a liverwort) **9**:532

Mimosa pudica (Sensitive or Humble plant) **9:568–569**

NOP

Nuphar lutea (spatterdock) **16**:980

Nymphaea alba (White water lily) **16**:980

Olea europaea (European olive tree) **10**:638, 639

Oryza sativa (rice) **13:780–781**

Palmaria palmata (dulse) **8**:483

Papaver nudicaule (Iceland poppy) **12**:718

Papaver radicatum (Arctic poppy) **10**:598; **12:718–719**

Papaver rhoeas (Corn poppy) **4**:233; **12**:718

Papaver somniferum (Opium poppy) **12**:718, 719

Passiflora spp. (passionflowers) **11:678–679**

Pellia epiphylla (a liverwort) **9**:532

Peniocereus greggi (Queen-of-the-night) **3**:138

Persea americana (avocado) **1:48–49**

Phoenix dactylifera (Date palm) **11**:670, 671

Phoradendron serotinum (North American mistletoe) **9**:573

Pinus parviflora (Japanese white pine) **2**:116

Pinus sylvestris (Scot's pine) **12**:716

Pitcairnia feliciana (a bromeliad) **2**:122

Pleurozia purpurea (a liverwort) **9**:532

Psilotum spp. (whisk fern) **16:1000–1001**

Puya raimondii (puya) **2**:122, 123

QR

Quercus suber (Cork oak) **10**:624–625

Radula complanata (a liverwort) **9**:532

Rafflesia arnoldii (Monster flower) **12:754–755**

Ranunculus montanus (Mountain buttercup) **10**:599

Volume numbers are in **boldface type** followed by colons. Page numbers in **boldface type** indicate full articles.

Raphia ruffia (Raffia palm) **11**:670

Ravenala madagascariensis (Traveler's palm) **2**:101

Rhapidophyllum hystrix (Needle palm) **11**:670–671

Rhizophora mangle (Red or American mangrove) **9**:552–553

Rhizophora mangle (Red mangrove) **16**:992

Rosa spp. (rose) **13**:**786–787**

Rosa x damascena (Damask rose) **13**:786, 787

S

Sabal paletto (Cabbage palmetto) **11**:671

Saccharum officinarum (sugarcane) **14**:**884–885**

Salix arctica (Arctic willow) **12**:717

Salix babylonica (Weeping willow) **16**:1006, 1007

Salix discolor (Pussy willow) **16**:1006, 1007

Salix polans (Polar willow) **12**:716

Sanguinaria canadensis (a poppy) **12**:719

Sarracenia purpurea (Purple or Common pitcher plant) **11**:702

Scapania nemorea (a liverwort) **9**:532

Schistostega pennata (Luminous moss) **10**:593

Sequoiadendron giganteum (Giant sequoia) **13**:816, 817

Sequoia sempervirens (Coast redwood) **13**:816, 817

Sesamum orientale (sesame) **13**:**818–819**

Sinapis alba (White mustard) **10**:610–611

Solanum lycopersicum (tomato plant) **15**:**932–933**

Solanum nigrum (Common or Black nightshade) **4**:241

Solanum scabrum (Garden huckleberry) **4**:241

Solanum tuberosum (potato) **4**:241; **12**:**724–725**

Sphaeralcea ambigua (Desert mallow) **4**:247

Sphagnum spp. (Peat or Bog moss) **10**:593

Strelitzia reginae (Bird-of-paradise flower or Crane flower) **2**:**101–102**

Syzygium aromaticum **5**:303

T

Taraxacum spp. (dandelion) **4**:**238–239**

Taxodium distichum (Bald cypress) **16**:990, 992

Tecona grandis (teak) **12**:759

Thuja occidentalis (White cedar) **16**:992

Tillandsia usneoides (Spanish moss) **2**:123

Trachycarpus fortunei (Windmill palm) **11**:670

Tribulus cistoides (Caltrop bush) **8**:469

Triticum spp. (wheat) **16**:**998–999**

Typha angustifolia (Narrow-leaved cattail) **3**:156

Typha latifolia (Common cattail) **3**:156, 157

UV

Ulva lactuca (sea lettuce) **1**:25; **15**:926

Urtica dioica (stinging nettle) **14**:**874–875**

Urtica ferox (a stinging nettle) **14**:875

Utricularia minor (Lesser bladderwort) **2**:108

Vanilla planifolia (Mexican or Bourbon vanilla) **11**:650, 651

Victoria amazonica (Amazon water lily) **16**:**980–981**

Viscum album (European mistletoe) **9**:572, 573

Viscum minimum (a mistletoe) **9**:573

Vitis rotundifolia (Muscadine grape) **6**:380

Vitis vinifera (European grape) **6**:380, 381

WXY

Welwitschia mirabilis (a gnetophyte) **6**:366; **16**:**988–989**

Yucca spp. (yucca) **16**:**1020–102**

Yucca brevifolia (Joshua tree) **16**:1020, 1021

Z

Zea mays (corn or maize) **4**:**212–213**; **6**:346

Zea mexicana (teosinte) **4**:212

Zizania aquatica (wild rice) **13**:780

Zostera marina (eelgrass) **16**:991

Other kingdoms

AB

Agaricus brunnescens (Edible mushroom) **6**:346

Amanita muscaria (Fly agaric) **6**:344, 345, 347

Amanita phalloides (Death cap toadstool) **6**:347

Amoeba proteus (an amoeba) **1**:30, 31

Aspergillus fumigatus (a fungus) **6**:346

C–F

Calvatia gigantea (Giant puffball) **6**:346, 347

Dactyella bembicodes (a fungus) **6**:345–346

Entamoeba gingivalis (an amoeba) **1**:31

Entamoeba histolytica (an amoeba) **1**:31

Escherichia coli (a bacterium) **1**:57

G–L

Gonyaulax catanella (a dinoflagellate) **1**:24, 25

Lactobacillus bulgaricus (a bacterium) **1**:59

Leucocoprinus gongylophorus (a fungus) **6**:346, 347

O–R

Ophiostoma novo-ulmi (a fungus) **6**:345, 346

Penicillium spp. (a fungus) **6**:345, 347

Plasmodium spp. (a protozoan) **3**:174–175

ST

Saccharomyces cerevisiae (Baker's and Brewers' yeast) **6**:346

Salmonella enteritidis (a bacterium) **1**:56

Staphylococcus aureus (a bacterium) **1**:58

Tuber gibbosum (truffle) **6**:346

U–Z

Ustilago sp. (corn smut) **6**:346

Yersinia pestis (a bacterium) **5**:31

Volume numbers are in **boldface type** followed by colons. Page numbers in **boldface type** indicate full articles.

Comprehensive Index

aardvark **1:14–15**

abyss **10**:629

acacia **1:16–17; 6**:364; **9**:569; **13**:802–803

acacia ant **1**:16, 17

acorn squash **14**:865

acorn woodpecker **16**:1015

adder **15**:903

adjutant stork **14**:877

aestivation **4**:248; **7**:419; **9**:541

   See also hibernation

African buffalo **1:18–19; 11**:668

African chameleon **3**:160, 161

African donkey **5**:264–265

African dormouse **5**:267

African elephant **5**:292, 293, 294

African fish eagle **5**:279, 280

African golden mole **4**:249

African gray parrot **11**:677

African jacana **8**:471

African lungfish **9**:540–541

African oryx (gemsbok) **11**:656, 657

African rock python **12**:742

African wild dog **1:20–21; 4**:255; **16**:1005

agar **1**:24

agile wallaby **16**:972, 973

agouti **1**:32; **2**:121

Albany pitcher plant **11**:702

albatross **1:22–23**

albinos **12**:761

alder **2**:96; **10**:598; **15**:945

alevins **13**:797

alga **1:24–25**

   fungus-alga association

     See lichen

   marine **1**:24–25; **8**:482–483

     See also seaweed

algal blooms **1**:24, 25

algin **8**:483

alkaloids **3**:175; **4**:241; **12**:719

Allen's galago **6**:349

alligator **1:26–27**, 32; **10**:608; 16:993

   American **1**:26, 27; **16**:993

Alligator turtle **15**:950

almond tree **13**:786

aloe **1:28–29**

alpaca **3**:145; **9**:534, 535

Alpine bearberry **15**:944

Alpine forget-me-not **10**:598

altitude, and temperature **10**:598

Amazon water lily **16**:980–981

American alligator **1**:26, 27; **16**:993

American avocet **1**:50–51

American badger **1**:60–61

American basswood **15**:915

American bollworm **4**:215

American bullfrog **6**:340, 341, 342; **15**:930

American butterfly **12**:757

American cockroach **3**:185; **15**:955

American coot **4**:204–205

American cowbird **4**:231

American crocodile **4**:226, 227; **16**:993

American crow **4**:228

American elk (wapiti) **4**:244; **5:298–299**

American goldfinch **6**:370, 371

American holly **7**:430, 431

American (Northern) jacana **8**:470, 471

American kestrel **8**:484, 485; **14**:855

American (North Atlantic) lobster **9**:536, 537

American (Red) mangrove **9**:552–553; **16**:992

American mink **9**:570, 571; **15**:903

American moon moth **10**:596

American pine marten **11**:696, 697

American (Common) raven **12**:764, 765

American robin **13**:784–785

American toad **15**:930, 931

American white pelican **11**:684–685

American (Carolina) wood duck **5**:272, 274–275

ammocoetes **8**:505

amoeba **1:30–31**

amphibians

   tailed **1**:52–53; **13**:794–795

   tailless **6**:340–343; **15**:930–931

anaconda **1:32–33**

Andean condor **4**:202–203

Andean sword-billed hummingbird **7**:446–447

Andes Mountains **10**:598; **13**:803

Andrew's frigate bird **6**:339

anemone, sea *See* sea anemone

angelfish **1:34–35**

angiosperms *See* flowering plants

angler fish **1:36–37**

angleworm (earthworm) **5:282–283; 14**:882

Angolan impala **8**:467

Anjouan scops owl **11**:667

annelids **5**:282

annual plants **6**:336; **12**:719

   desert **4**:247

   grasses **6**:382

ant **1:38–39**

   Acacia **1**:16, 17

   bull **16**:971

   carpenter **1**:40

   leaf-cutting **1**:38, 39; **6**:346, 347

Antarctic **12**:717

Antarctic cod **10**:629

antbear (aardvark) **1:14–15**

anteater **1:40–41**

Banded (numbat) **10:618–619**

   Spiny **5**:286, 287

antelope(s) **1:42–43; 16**:1023

   East African giraffe **6**:352

   See also dik-dik; eland; impala; nilgai; saiga; springbok; wildebeest

antennae

   cockroach **3**:184

   lobster **9**:536, 537

   moth and butterfly **10**:594, 597

antifreeze **12**:716; **15**:945

antlers **4**:242–243, 244

   caribou **3**:150–151

   elk **5**:298

   moose **10**:588, 589

   sambar **13**:798, 799

ants **1**:14; **11**:674–675

ape(s) **3**:168–169; **6**:358–359, 376–377; **11**:648–649

   Barbary **2:72–73**

aphids **8**:498; **14**:882

Appalachian Mountains **15**:915

apple **13**:786

Arabian camel (Dromedary) **3**:142, 144–145; **4**:248

Arabian coffee **4**:198

Arabian oryx **11**:656

Arabian tahr **6**:369

aracari **15**:936, 937

arachnids **2**:106–107; **13**:800–801; **14**:856–859; **15**:908–909

Arboreal salamander **13**:794–795

Arctic **12**:716–717

Arctic fox **15**:945

Arctic ground squirrel **15**:945

Arctic (Mountain) hare **7**:412–413; **15**:945

Arctic (Collared) lemming **8**:508, 509

Arctic loon **9**:538

Arctic poppy **10**:598; **12**:718–719

Arctic redpoll **12**:716

Arctic tern **15**:922, 923, 945

Arctic willow **12**:717

Volume numbers are in **boldface type** followed by colons.
Page numbers in **boldface type** indicate full articles.

armadillo **1**:40, **44–45**

arrack **11**:671

Arrow poison frog **6**:342, 343

arrowroot **4**:237

arthropods **7**:442–443

arum **1**:**46–47**

asexual reproduction, in starfish **14**:871

Asian black bear **2**:82, 84–85

Asian brown mustard **10**:611

Asian donkey **5**:264–265

Asian elephant **5**:294, 295

Asiatic chipmunk **3**:171

asparagus **9**:523; **14**:860

aspen **16**:1007

aspergillosis **6**:346

aspirin **16**:1006

Assam tea **15**:712, 713

aster **14**:888

Desert **4**:247

Atlantic cod **3**:188, 189

Atlantic halibut **7**:408

Atlantic manta ray **12**:766, 767

Atlantic Ocean **10**:626, 627

Atlantic puffin **12**:738, 739

Atlantic salmon **13**:796, 797

Atlantic sturgeon **14**:880, 881

Atlantic torpedo ray **12**:767

Atlas moth **10**:597

atropine **4**:241

attar **13**:787

Attwater's prairie chicken **12**:727

Auckland Island merganser **9**:565

auk **12**:**716–717**

aureomycin **1**:59

Australian bustard **2**:126

Australian lungfish **9**:540, 541

Australian sea wasp **8**:476

Austrian (Woolly) foxglove **6**:337

Austrian pine **11**:695

avocado **1**:**48–49**

avocet **1**:**50–51**

axolotl **1**:**52–53**

aye-aye **8**:510

B

baboon **1**:**54–55**

See also mandrill

Bacillus bacteria **1**:58

bacteria **1**:**56–59**

fossil **10**:626

sulphur **10**:627–628, 629

Bactrian camel **3**:142, 143, 144; **4**:248

badger **1**:**60–61**; **15**:917

American **1**:60–61

Honey **1**:60, 61; **7**:**432–433**; **14**:863

Baikal, Lake **8**:500–501, 503

Baird's tapir **15**:906

Baker's yeast **6**:346

Bald cypress **13**:816; **16**:990, 992

Bald eagle **5**:278, 279; **11**:658; **16**:993

Bald (White or Red) uakari **15**:952, 953

baleen plates **10**:628; **16**:996

Baltimore oriole **11**:652, 653

bamboo **1**:**62–63**; **11**:672, 673

banana **2**:101

Banana slug **14**:847

bandages, mosses as **10**:593

Banded anteater (numbat) **10**:**618–619**

Banded garden spider **14**:856, 857

Banded mongoose **10**:585

bandicoot, Gunn's **7**:**406–407**

banksia **2**:**70–71**

bank vole **16**:966, 967

Banyan tree **5**:311

Barbary ape (Barbary macaque) **2**:**72–73**

Barbary sheep **6**:368

barbels **3**:154; **8**:502; **14**:880

bark

of cork oak **10**:624–625

of eucalypts **5**:303

barley **6**:382

barnacle **15**:**926–927**

Barnacle goose **6**:374

Barn owl **11**:664, 665

Barn swallow **14**:890, 891

barracuda **2**:**74–75**; **4**:211

Basking shark **13**:822

bass **2**:**76–77**

bat **2**:**78–81**, 100; **3**:139;

6:328–329

bay **15**:915

Baya weaverbird **16**:986

bay owl **11**:666

beak *See* bill/beak

beans, coffee **4**:199

Bearded seal **12**:714

Beard lichen **9**:521

bear(s) **2**:**82–85**; **11**:672–673; **15**:917; **16**:1010

Black **2**:83, 84; **5**:298; **15**:903

Brown **2**:82, 83–84; **15**:903

Grizzly **2**:82, 83–84; **5**:298

Polar bear **2**:82, 83; **12**:**714–715**

beaver **2**:**86–87**; **15**:903; **16**:991

bedbug **3**:172

bee **2**:**88–89**

bee-eater **2**:**90–91**

beetle **2**:**92–93**; **16**:981

dung **2**:92, 93; **7**:**392–393**

elm-bark **6**:345

Firefly **5**:**312–313**

ladybug **8**:**498–499**; **14**:882

Tenebrionid **4**:249

Beisa oryx (gemsbok) **11**:656, 657

belladonna (Deadly nightshade) **4**:**240–241**; **12**:724; **15**:932

Belted kingfisher **8**:488, 489

beluga (White whale) **14**:881; **16**:995, 996

Berried sea anemone **13**:805

berries **7**:417

cacti **3**:139

Deadly nightshade **4**:240, 241

Holly **7**:430, 431

mangrove **9**:552, 553

mistletoe **9**:572

biennial plants **6**:336; **7**:420

Bighorn sheep **2**:**94–95**; **10**:599

bilberry **10**:598

bill/beak

albatross **1**:23

avocet **1**:50

bird of paradise **2**:99

blackbird **2**:102–103

Blue jay **2**:112–113

cardinal **3**:148

casques **7**:434–435

cockatoo **3**:183

curlew **4**:234

Darwin's finches **8**:469

flamingo **5**:314

gull **7**:404

hornbill **7**:434–435

hummingbird **7**:446

ibis **8**:463

limpkin **9**:526

oxpecker **11**:669

parrot **9**:544–545; **11**:676

pelican **11**:684, 685

pigeon **5**:269

platypus **12**:710–711

shoebill **13**:824, 825

stork **14**:877

storm petrel **11**:690

sunbird **14**:886

toucan **15**:936

billfish **9**:556

bioluminescence **10**:629

birch **2**:**96–97**; **6**:345; **12**:716; **15**:945

birchmouse **10**:600, 603

bird-eating spider **15**:909

bird of paradise **2**:**98–99**

Bird-of-paradise flower (Crane flower) **2**:**100–101**

bird(s)

diving *See* diving birds

flightless *See* flightless birds

game *See* game birds

garden **14**:883

grassland **2**:126–127; **7**:393

perching *See* perching birds

suburban **14**:883

temperate forest **15**:916–917

urban **15**:954–955

wading *See* wading birds

See also birds of prey; cuckoo family; hornbills; hummingbird family; parrots; seabirds; toucan family; waterbirds; waterfowl; woodpecker family

Bird's nest fern **5**:307

Volume numbers are in **boldface type** followed by colons. Page numbers in **boldface type** indicate full articles.

rds of prey **4**:202–203;
  5:278–281, 304–305;
  7:414–415; **8**:484–485;
  11:658–659, 664–667;
  13:814–815; **14**:854–855;
  16:968–969
son
  American (buffalo) **2:124–125**
  European (wisent) **1**:18–19;
    2:125
tter aloe **1**:29
ttern **16**:993
valve mollusks **3**:176–177
ack-and-white colobus monkey
  4:200, 201
ack-backed (Silver-backed) jackal
  8:472
ack bear **2**:83, 84; **5**:298;
  15:903
ackbird **2:102–103**
ackbuck **2:104–105**
ack-capped chickadee **3**:166, 167
ack cayman **1**:27
ack-faced impala **8**:467
ack-footed ferret **5**:308–309;
  12:728–729; **16**:984
ack-headed uakari **15**:952
ack-headed weaver **16**:987
ack lion tamarin **15**:904
ack marlin **9**:556, 557
ack mustard **10**:611
ack pine **11**:695
ack (Roof) rat **10**:600–601;
  12:760–761
ack rhinoceros **13**:777–778, 779
ack salmon **13**:797
ack-shouldered opossum **11**:646
ack-spored quillwort **12**:749
ack-striped wallaby **16**:973
ack swan **14**:892
ack-tailed jackrabbit **12**:750, 751
ck-tailed prairie dog **12**:728
ack widow spider **2:106–107;**
  14:858
ack wildebeest **16**:1005
ck willow **16**:1006
ck woodpecker **16**:1015
dderwort **2:108–109,** 122–123
nny, Mimic **16**:1016
ght, late **12**:725

Blood star **14**:870, 871
blooms, algal **1**:24, 25
blowfish **12**:736
blowfly **5**:318
blubber **13**:808, 811
Blue-and-yellow macaw **9**:544
Blue angelfish **1**:35
bluebell **9**:523; **15**:916
bluebird **2:110–111**
Blue catfish **3**:154
Bluefin tuna **10**:629; **15**:942, 943
blue-green alga **1**:59; **10**:626, 627
Blue (Arctic) hare **7**:412–413
Blue jay **2:112–113**
Blue marlin **9**:557
Blue mussel **15**:926
Blue-ringed octopus **10**:634, 635
Blue scarab **2**:92
Blue Streak (Cleaner wrasse)
  4:211; **7**:399; **16**:1016, 1017
Blue-striped pipefish **11**:699
Blue tit **3**:167
Blue whale **10**:628–629; **13**:816;
  16:994, 995, 996, 997
Blue wildebeest **16**:1004–1005
Boa constrictor **1**:32
boas **1**:32, 33
Boat-tailed grackle **6**:378, 379
bobcat **2:114–115; 9**:519
Bobwhite quail (Northern
  bobwhite) **12**:744, 745
Bog onion (jack-in-the pulpit)
  1:46–47
bogs **16**:991
Bolas spider **14**:858
bollworm **4**:215
bonito **15**:942–943
bonobo (Pygmy chimpanzee)
  3:168, 169
bonsai **2:116–117**
bony fish **5**:288–289; **9**:540–541;
  10:604–605; **13**:796–797;
  14:880–881; **15**:940–941
  freshwater **3**:152–155;
    11:688–689, 700–701
  saltwater **1**:34–37; **2**:74–77;

3:188–191; **6**:326–327;
  7:398–399, 408–409,
  426–427; **9**:530–531,
  556–557; **10**:630–631;
  11:698–699; **12**:736–737;
  13:806–807; **15**:942–943;
  16:1016–1017
booming grounds **12**:726
Boreal chickadee **3**:167
Botany bay kino **5**:302
Botta's pocket gopher **12**:713
Bottle gourd **14**:864
Bottlenose dolphin **5**:262, 263
Bourbon (Mexican) vanilla **11**:650,
  651
bowerbird **2:118–119**
bowers **2**:118–119
"boxing"
  by hares **7**:413
  by kangaroos **8**:478
bracken fern **5**:307
bracts **2**:123; **4**:238; **11**:671
brain coral **4**:208
bran, rice **13**:781
Brazilian merganser **9**:565
Brazilian rubber tree **13:788–789**
Brazilian (South American) tapir
  15:906, 907
Brazil nut tree **2:120–121**
breeding, selective **9**:523, 554
Brewer's blackbird **2**:102, 103
Brewer's yeast **6**:346
Brindled gnu (Blue wildebeest)
  16:1004–1005
Brindled nailtail wallaby
  16:972–973
brittle star **10**:629
brocket **4**:245
"broken wing act" **8**:487
brolga **4**:221
bromeliad **2:122–123**
Brook lamprey **8**:504
brown algae **1**:24
Brown bark **3**:175
Brown bear **2**:82, 83–84; **15**:903
Brown bullhead **3**:155

Brown creeper **15**:917
Brown-headed nuthatch **10**:621
Brown hyena **8**:457
Brown kiwi **8**:490, 491
Brown lemming **8**:509
Brown lemur **8**:510
Brown locust **7**:391
Brown long-eared bat **2**:81
Brown pelican **11**:684, 685
Brown (Common) rat
  10:600–601; **12**:760, 761;
  15:954
Brown recluse spider **14**:858
Brown thrasher **13**:785
Brown trout **15**:941
Brush wolf *See* coyote
bryophytes *See* liverwort; moss
Bubbler crab **4**:218
Buckeye butterfly **3**:137
budding, by hydra **8**:455
budgerigar **11**:676, 677
buffalo **2:124–125; 15**:929
  African **1:18–19; 11**:668
bug
  lightning (firefly) **5:312–313**
  lygus **4**:215
Bulb-bearing lily **9**:523
bulbs, lily **9**:522, 523
bull ant **16**:971
Bull banksia **2**:70
Bull bay (Southern magnolia)
  9:546, 547
bullfrog, American **6**:340, 341,
  342; **15**:930
Bullock's oriole **11**:652, 653
Bull's horn acacia **1:16–17**
bunting **3**:148; **14**:852
Burchell's zebra **7**:392
Burmeister's porpoise **12**:723
bur reed **16**:991
burrfish **12**:737
Burrowing owl **11**:667; **12**:729
Burrowing toad **15**:931
burrows
  aardvark **1**:14
  armadillo **1**:44
  badger **1**:60
  chipmunk **3**:171
  earthworm **5**:283
  groundhog **7**:397

burrows (continued)
  kingfisher **8**:489
  luminous mosses in **10**:593
  Marsupial mole **9**:560–561
  muskrat **10**:609
  petrel **11**:691
  platypus **12**:711
  pocket gopher **12**:712–713
  prairie dog **12**:728, 729
  puffin **12**:739
  vole **16**:966
  wombat **16**:1012
bushbaby (galago) **6**:348–349
bustard **2**:126–127
Butter clam **3**:177
butterfly **3**:134–137; **10**:594
  American **12**:757
  differs from moths **10**:594
  Holly blue **7**:431
  Red admiral **14**:875
butterfly fish (lionfish) **1**:35;
  4:211; **9**:530–531
  Thread fin **7**:398–399
butternut squash **14**:864
butterwort **2**:109
buttress roots **12**:757

C
Cabbage palmetto **11**:671
cacao **14**:884
Cackling goose **6**:374
cactus **3**:138–139; **4**:247; **12**:751
caddis fly **3**:140–141
caffeine **4**:199; **15**:913
caffeol **4**:199
cajeput oil **5**:303
California barracuda **2**:75
California condor **4**:203
Californian poppy **12**:718, 719
California pitcher plant (Cobra
  lily) **11**:702–703
California sea lion **13**:810–811
Caltrop bush **8**:469
camel **3**:142–145; **4**:248, 249
camelids **3**:145
camouflage
  Arctic hare **7**:412
  bustard **2**:126
  butterfly **3**:137
  chameleon **3**:160, 161

crab **4**:218, 219
dolphin **5**:262
fish **3**:153
flying lemur **6**:331
grasshopper **7**:390
grouse **7**:400
halibut **7**:409
okapi **10**:636, 637
praying mantis **12**:731
ruff **13**:791
viper **15**:959
Canada goose **6**:372, 374, 375
Canadian beaver **2**:86, 87
Canadian jay **2**:113
Canadian lynx **9**:542
Canadian porcupine **12**:721
canines **11**:682; **16**:974, 976
Cannonball tree **2**:120, 121
Cape buffalo **1**:18, 19
Cape hunting dog (African wild
  dog) **1**:20–21
Cape jasmine **3**:175
Cape Mountain cockroach **3**:184
Cape pangolin **11**:674, 675
capercaillie **15**:903
Cape rock hyrax **8**:458
Cape vulture **16**:968
caprifig **5**:311
capsules
  fruit **9**:522
  spore **9**:533; **12**:749
capuchin-like monkey **10**:614
capuchin monkey **10**:614
capybara **3**:146–147
caracara **13**:774
carapace **4**:218; **14**:856;
  15:924–925, 934, 948–949
cardinal
  Northern **3**:148–149; **14**:883
  Red **14**:852
Cardinal fish **13**:813
Caribbean pitch pine **11**:695
caribou **3**:150–151; **9**:521;
  15:945; **16**:1009
  European (reindeer) **3**:151;
  4:243; **9**:521

Carmine bee-eater **2**:91
carnivorous flowering plants *See*
  flowering plants, carnivorous
Carolina chickadee **3**:167
Carolina (American) wood duck
  5:272, 274–275
carp **3**:152–153
carpenter ant **1**:40
carrier pigeon **5**:268
cartilage **12**:766
cartilaginous fish *See* ray; shark
Caspian Sea **8**:502, 503
castor oil plant **13**:788
Cat bear (Red panda) **11**:672, 673
catbird **16**:992
  Gray **9**:574
caterpillars **3**:134, 135, 136, 137;
  4:215, 233; **10**:597; **14**:839,
  882
  hornworms **10**:594–595
catfish **3**:154–155
  Sharptooth **8**:503
catkins **2**:96–97, 97; **10**:624;
  14:874; **16**:1006, 1007
cat(s) **2**:114–115; **3**:164–165;
  8:474–475; **9**:518–519,
  528–529, 542–543;
  10:632–633; **12**:740–741;
  15:928–929; **16**:1002–1003
cattail **3**:156–157; **16**:991
cattle
  domestic **1**:18
  and the Screwworm fly **5**:319
  the "wobbles" **4**:237
  See also bison; buffalo; Musk
    ox; yak
Cattle egret **7**:425
cave **3**:158–159
  luminous mosses **10**:593
cavernicoles (troglodytes)
  3:158–159
Cave salamander (manfish) **3**:158,
  159
Cave swiftlet **3**:159
caviar **14**:881
cavy (guinea pig) **7**:402–403

cayman **1**:26, 27, 33; **10**:623;
  16:993
cell eating **1**:30
cell membrane **1**:56
cellulose **4**:200
cell wall **1**:56
Chacma baboon **1**:54
Chacoan peccary **11**:683
chameleon **3**:160–161
chamois **3**:162–163; **10**:599
Channel catfish **3**:154
chaparral **13**:803
charcoal **11**:695
cheek pouches **7**:411; **8**:481;
  12:713
cheese **1**:59
cheetah **3**:164–165
chelonians *See* terrapin; tortoise;
  turtle
chemicals, for defense **9**:567
cherry **15**:915
Cherry birch **2**:96
Chestnut-backed chickadee **3**:167
chickadee **3**:166–167
chicory **4**:239
Chihuahuan raven **12**:764
Chilean fire bush **2**:70
Chile strawberry **14**:878
Chimney swift **14**:883, 894, 895
chimpanzee **3**:168–169
China grass **14**:874
Chinese alligator **1**:26
Chinese pangolin **11**:675
Chinese praying mantis **12**:731
Chinese silkworm **14**:838–839
chipmunk **3**:170–171
chital **4**:243, 244
chlorophyll **2**:96
chrysalis **3**:134, 135, 136
chrysanthemum **14**:888
Chuckwalla **8**:465
cicada **3**:172–173
cilia **14**:870
Cinnamon fern **5**:307
cinchona **3**:174–175
cinchonine **3**:175
Cinnamon bear **2**:84
clam **3**:176–177; **15**:927
cleanerfish (Cleaner wrasse) **4**:21
  5:288; **7**:399; **16**:1016, 1017

Volume numbers are in **boldface type** followed by colons.
Page numbers in **boldface type** indicate full articles.

eaner wrasse **4**:211; **5**:288; **7**:399; **16**:1016, 1017

tellum **5**:283

oacae **1**:33; **13**:795

louded leopard **9**:519

ownfish **4**:211; **13**:805

own shrimp **13**:828

ub moss **3:178–179; 12**:748

oalfish **3**:189

oarse-haired (Common) wombat **16**:1013

ast, tide pool and **15:926–927**

past redwood **13**:816, 817

obra **3:180–181**

obra lily (California pitcher plant) **11:702–703**

occus bacteria **1**:58

ochineal beetle **2**:93

ckatiel **3**:182, 183

ckatoo **3:182–183**

ckle **15**:927

ckroach **3:184–185; 10**:590
 American **15**:955

oconut palm **3:186–187; 11**:671

conuts **3**:186, 187

coons
 earthworm **5**:283
 silkworm **14**:838, 839
 See also pupae/pupation

d **3:188–189; 10**:629

deine **12**:719

elacanth **3:190–191**

ffee **4:198–199**

ffee leaf rust **4**:199

ir **3**:187

llared anteater **1**:41

ollared lemming **8**:508, 509

ollared peccary **11:682–683**

lobus monkey **4:200–201; 12**:732

onies
 coral **4**:206–209
 frigate bird **6**:339
 gull **7**:405
 penguin **11**:686, 687
 weaver **16**:987

lor
 changing **3**:160, 161; **14**:867
 defense **1**:35
 warning **14**:842

See also camouflage

Colorado beetle **2**:92–93

colt **7**:440

colugo (flying lemur) **6:330–331**

Common baboon **1**:54

Common (Feathery) bamboo **1**:62–63

Common carp **3**:152, 153

Common cattail **3**:156, 157

Common chimpanzee **3**:168, 169

Common (Atlantic) cod **3**:188, 189

Common (European) coot **4**:204, 205

Common (European) cuckoo **4**:230, 231

Common (Eurasian) curlew **4**:235

Common dolphin **5**:262, 263; **16**:994

Common earthworm **5**:282

Common earwig **5**:284, 285

Common eider **5**:275

Common fig **5**:311

Common (Purple) foxglove **6**:336–337

Common frog **6**:340, 342

Common gallinule (moorhen) **4**:205; **6**:350

Common grackle **6**:378, 379

Common hammerhead **13**:820

Common hamster **7**:410–411

Common hedgehog **7**:418, 419

Common herring **7**:426

Common horsetail **7**:444

Common iguana **8**:464–465

Common jay **2**:113

Common kestrel **8**:484

Common kingfisher **8**:488

Common (Brown) kiwi **8**:490, 491

Common long-nosed armadillo **1**:44–45

Common loon **9**:539

Common marmoset **9**:559

Common merganser **9**:564, 565

Common midwife toad **15**:931

Common (Gray) moorhen **6**:351

Common musk turtle **15**:949

Common nightingale **10**:612–613

Common octopus **10**:634–635

Common (Virginia) opossum **11**:646–647; **15**:955

Common peacock **11**:680, 681

Common (Ring-necked) pheasant **11**:692, 693

Common (Purple) pitcher plant **11**:702

Common puffin **12**:738, 739

Common quail **12**:744

Common (North American) raccoon **12**:752, 753; **15**:955

Common (Brown) rat **10**:600–601; **12**:760, 761; **15**:954

Common raven **12**:764, 765

Common rhea **13**:774, 775

Common (Edible) sea urchin **13**:812, 813

Common shrimp **13**:828, 829

Common (Striped) skunk **14**:842–843

Common snapping turtle **15**:950

Common (European) starling **14**:872, 873

Common (Tailless) tenrec **15**:918–919

Common toad **15**:903

Common vampire bat **2**:79, 80, 81

Common vole **16**:967

Common wasp **16**:978

Common (Coarse-haired) wombat **16**:1013

Common yellow dung fly **5**:318

Common (Plains) zebra **16**:1022–1023

condor **4:202–203**

cone-bearing plants **6**:362–363, 366–367

woody *See* woody plants, with cones

cones
 cycad **4**:237

ginko **6**:363

gnetophyte **6**:367; **16**:989

horsetail **7**:445

larch **8**:506, 507

pine **11**:694, 695

sequoia **13**:817

Congo coffee **4**:198

conifers **11:694–695**
 of the taiga **15:902–903**

coniine **7**:420

continental shelf **7**:426, 427

coot **4:204–205; 16**:993

coral **4:206–209**

coral islands **8**:468

coral reef **4**:206, 209, **210–211, 219; 8**:468
 cleaning stations **7**:399
 fish **1**:34–35; **4**:208, 210–211; **9**:530–531

cordgrass **16**:991

cork **10**:624, 625

Cork oak **10:624–625**

corkscrew-shaped bacillus **1**:59

corm **1**:46; **12**:748

corn (maize) **4:212–213; 6**:346

corn borer **4**:213, 215

Corn earworm **4**:213, 215

Corn marigold **4**:233

Corn poppy **4**:233

Corn smut **6**:346

corolla **7**:417

corona **11**:678

cotton **4:214–215**

cottonmouth **16:982–983**

cotton rat **4**:215

Cotton-top tamarin **15**:905

cotyledons **6**:383; **9**:522

cougar *See* puma

counting, by birds **4**:228

courtship displays
 alligator **1**:26–27
 bird **1**:51; **2**:119, 127; **5**:269, 280, 315; **6**:338, 339, 378–379; **7**:395, 415, 424–425; **8**:485; **9**:564–565; **10**:612–613; **11**:658–659, 661, 680–681, 693; **12**:726, 727, 735, 747; **13**:775, 815; **14**:855; **15**:947

Volume numbers are in **boldface type** followed by colons. Page numbers in **boldface type** indicate full articles.

cowbird 2:103; 4:231; 11:655
Cow parsley 7:421
coyote 1:44, 61; 4:216–217;
    10:608; 12:713, 728–729;
    14:883; 16:1011
crab 4:218–219; 15:926, 927
    fiddler 16:991
    hermit 7:422–423; 13:805
    Horseshoe (King) 7:442–443
Crab-eating raccoon 12:752
crane 4:220–221
Crane (Bird-of-paradise) flower
    2:100–101
crane fly 4:222–223
Crane hawk 7:414–415
Crested myna 14:873
Crested oropendola 11:654, 655
crested porcupine 12:720
Crestless gardener bowerbird
    2:118
Cretan maple 9:554
cricket 4:224–225
crocodile 1:26; 4:226–227;
    10:587; 16:993
    American 4:226, 227; 16:993
crocodilians 1:26–27; 4:226–227
crookneck squash 14:864
crop milk 5:268, 315
crops
    and the Colorado beetle 2:93
    and the rhea 13:775
    See also corn; cotton; cultivated
        land; rice; sesame; soybean;
        sunflower; wheat
cross-breeding 14:878
cross-pollination 6:380
crow 4:228–229
Crowned crane 4:221
Crown-of-thorns starfish 4:209,
    211
crustaceans 4:218–219; 7:422–423;
    9:536–537; 13:828–829
Cuban bee hummingbird 7:446
Cuban crow 4:228
cuckoo 2:103; 4:230–231
cuckoo family 4:230–231;
    13:782–783
Cuckoo weaver 16:987
Cucumber tree 9:547
culms 1:62; 6:383

cultivated land 4:232–233
    See also crops
Cultivated strawberry 14:879
curlew 4:234–235; 15:945
cuticle (plant) 3:138; 4:247
cuttlebone 14:867
cuttlefish 14:867
cycad 4:236–237
cypress swamps 16:992
cysts, amoeboid 1:30–31

D
dace 8:502
daddy longlegs (cranefly)
    4:222–223
dahlia 14:888
Dahurian larch 15:902–903
dairy farming 4:233
daisy 14:888, 889
Dall's porpoise 12:722; 16:994
Damask rose 13:786, 787
dams, beaver 2:87
dance, of cranes 4:220–221
dance fly 5:319
dandelion 4:238–239; 14:888
darter dragonfly 5:270
Dartmoor pony 7:439
Darwin's rhea 13:775
dassie 8:458–459
Date palm 11:670, 671
day lily 9:523
Deadly nightshade (belladonna)
    4:240–241; 12:724; 15:932
Death cap toadstool 6:347
Death's head hawk moth 10:595
deciduous forests 15:914–915, 917
deciduous plants 2:96; 9:546, 554
decomposition 1:57–58
    forest decomposers 15:916
Decorator crab 4:218, 219
deer 4:242–245; 14:883; 15:917
    See also elk; sambar
deer (white-footed) mouse 10:600,
    602–603
deforestation 4:211
Desert aster 4:247

Desert buckwheat 13:803
Desert cavy 7:402
Desert dormouse 5:267
desert 4:246–249; 11:656
Desert holly 4:249
Desert locust 7:391
Desert mallow 4:247
Desert mesquite 4:247
Desert sand fox 4:249
Desert tarantula 15:908, 909
desman 10:582, 583
devilray (Atlantic manta ray)
    12:766, 767
dhole 4:250–251, 255
Diadem sea urchin 13:813
Diamond-back terrapin
    15:924–925; 16:991
diatoms 1:25
dicotyledons 6:383; 9:522
digitalis 4:241; 6:336
digoxin 6:337
dik-dik 4:252–253
dingo 4:254–255; 15:911
dinoflagellates 1:25
dioecious plants 6:367; 7:431;
    10:624
diplococcus 1:58
dipping duck 5:273
diseases, bacterial 1:57, 58
dispersal, fruit and seed 3:156,
    157; 4:239; 6:383; 12:719;
    14:879
display grounds See leks
displays, courtship See courtship
    displays
diurnal animals 11:662
diver 9:539
diving birds 9:538–539
dodo 5:269; 8:469
dog(s) 4:216–217, 250–251,
    254–255; 6:334–335;
    8:472–473; 16:1008–1011
    African wild 1:20–21; 4:255;
        16:1005
    Red or Whistling (dhole)
        4:250–251

dolphin 5:262–263; 16:994,
    996–997
Domestic cat 16:1002; 13:827
domestic cattle 1:18
Domestic guinea pig 7:402, 403
Domestic horse 7:439
Domestic turkey 15:946
donkey 5:264–265
dormancy, seed 4:247
dormouse 5:266–267; 10:600;
    15:917
dove 5:268–269
Dragon fish (lionfish) 4:211;
    9:530–531
dragonfly 5:270–271
dreaming 16:1017
dromedary 3:142, 144–145
drone (hover-) fly 5:319
drought 14:863
drugs
    illegal 12:719
    See also medicines and drugs
drupes 10:638; 11:671
duck 5:272–275
    See also merganser
Duck-billed platypus 12:710–711
dugong 5:276–277
dulse 8:483
dung beetle 2:92, 93; 7:392–393
Durango scorpion 13:801
Dusky dolphin 5:263
dusselfink 6:371
Dust Bowl 7:392
Dutch elm disease 6:346
Dwarf crocodile 4:226
Dwarf herring 7:427
Dwarf lemur 8:510, 511
dwarf mistletoe 9:573
Dwarf mongoose 10:584, 585
Dwarf sea horse 13:806, 807
dyes 9:521; 12:719
Dzungarian hamster 7:410

E
eagle 5:278–281; 14:863
    Bald 5:278, 279; 11:658
eagle owl 11:666
eared owl 11:666
ears, heat-loss from 4:248, 249
Earth pig (aardvark) 1:14–15

Volume numbers are in **boldface type** followed by colons.
Page numbers in **boldface type** indicate full articles.

rthworm **5:282–283; 14**:882

rwig **5:284–285**

rworm, Corn **4**:213, 215

st African giraffe antelope **6**:352

stern barred (Gunn's) bandicoot **7:406–407**

stern bluebird **2**:110, 111; **14**:873

stern chipmunk **3**:170, 171; **15**:916

stern cottontail rabbit **12**:750

stern fence lizard **8**:465

stern firefly **5**:312

stern gray squirrel **14**:868, 869; **15**:955

stern larch **8**:507

stern lowland gorilla **6**:376

stern mole **10**:582

st Indian fig **5**:311

hidna **5:286–287; 12**:710

hinoderms **13**:812–813; **14**:870–871

holocation

  bat **2**:78, 80; **3**:159

  dolphin **5**:263

  porpoise **12**:722

  swift **14**:895

  whale **16**:996

ema **6**:337

entates **1**:40

ible (Fat) dormouse **5**:266–267

ible frog **6**:340

ible-nest swiftlet **14**:895

ible sea urchin **13**:812, 813

 5:288–289

  Leopard moray **4**:211; **5**:288, 289

grass **9**:548; **16**:991

g-laying mammals **5**:286–287; **12**:710–711

gplant **12**:724; **15**:932

gs

  echidna **5**:287

  python **12**:743

  slug **14**:847

  turtle **15**:951

g tooth **1**:27

ret **11**:659; **16**:991, 993

  Cattle **7**:425

yptian cobra **3**:180, 181

yptian mongoose **10**:585

Egyptian vulture **16**:969

eiderdown **5**:275

Eider duck **5**:274, 275

eland **5:290–291**

Electric eel **5**:289

electric ray **12**:767

elephant **5:292–295**

elephant fern **5**:306

Elephant hawk moth **10**:594

elephant shrew **5:296–297**

elk **4**:244; **5:298–299; 12**:741

elm **6**:346; **14**:874

elm-bark beetle **6**:345

elvers **5**:289

elytra **5**:285

Emerald boa **1**:32

Emerald swallowtail butterfly **3**:134

Emperor angelfish **1**:34–35

Emperor dragonfly **5**:270, 271

Emperor of Germany's bird of paradise **2**:98

Emperor penguin **11**:686, 687; **12**:716

emu **5:300–301**

English (Common) starling **14**:872, 873

ephedrine **6**:367

epiphytes **2**:108, 122; **3**:178; **5**:310, 311; **12**:757

  orchids **11**:650

ermine **15**:945; **16**:984

Eskimo curlew **4**:235

estivation *See* aestivation

estuaries **8**:503; **10**:604; **16**:991

Estuarine (Saltwater) crocodile **4**:226

eubacteria **1**:58–59

eucalyptus **5:302–303; 8**:492, 493; **13**:803; **15**:915

euglenoids **1**:25

Eurasian avocet **1**:51

Eurasian (European) bee-eater **2**:90, 91

Eurasian (Common) curlew **4**:235

European bass **2**:77

European (Eurasian) bee-eater

2:90, 91

European bison **1**:18–19; **2**:125

European caribou (reindeer) **3**:151; **4**:243; **9**:521

European (African) chameleon **3**:160, 161

European (Common) coot **4**:204, 205

European corn poppy **12**:718

European (Common) cuckoo **4**:230, 231

European eel **5**:288–289

European grape **6**:380, 381

European jay **2**:113

European larch **8**:506–507

European lynx **9**:543

European mink **9**:571

European mistletoe **9**:572, 573

European mole **10**:582

European olive tree **10**:638, 639

European perch **11**:688

European pine marten **11**:696, 697

European pond terrapin **8**:502

European robin **13**:784, 785

European (Common) starling **14**:872, 873

European wild boar **16**:976

Everest, Mount **10**:599

Everglades **9**:527, 549, 552; **16**:990, 992–993

evergreen forests **15**:915

evergreen plants **9**:546, 554; **10**:624, 638

evolution **8**:468

exoskeleton **9**:566; **13**:828

extinct species

  birds **5**:269; **8**:469; **9**:565; **11**:677; **16**:1015

  tarpan **7**:441

Exxon Valdez disaster **11**:663

eyelids, third **7**:395; **11**:665

eyes

  compound **3**:141

  of tubers **12**:725

eye spots/eye-like patterns **10**:595; **12**:737

F

fairy rings **12**:755

fairy shrimp **13**:828

Falabella horse **7**:439

falcon **5:304–305**

  Peregrine **5**:304, 305; **15**:954–955

falconet **5**:304, 305

Fallow deer **4**:242, 243, 245

False cleaner **16**:1016

false feet **1**:30, 31

farmland *See* cultivated land

Fat (Edible) dormouse **5**:266–267

Fea's viper **15**:959

feathers

  bird of paradise **2**:98, 99

  duck **5**:272–273

  eating own **7**:395

  eiderdown **5**:275

  flamingo **5**:315

  flight **5**:272

  osprey **11**:659

  owl **11**:665

  peacock **11**:680–681

  penguin **11**:686

  ptarmigan **12**:734, 735

  quetzal **12**:746, 747

Feathery (Common) bamboo **1**:62–63

feet

  parrot **9**:545; **11**:676

  roadrunner **13**:782

  woodpecker **16**:1015

Fennec fox **4**:248

feral cat **16**:1002

fermentation **1**:59; **6**:381

fern **5:306–307**

fern group **3**:178–179; **5**:306–307; **7**:444–445; **12**:748–749; **16**:1000–1001

  See also club moss; fern; horsetail; quillwort; spike moss; whisk fern

ferret, Black-footed **5:308–309; 16**:984

fiddler crab **16**:991

Field vole **16**:966, 967

fig **5:310–311; 13**:803; **14**:874

Fig wasp **5**:310–311

Volume numbers are in **boldface type** followed by colons.
Page numbers in **boldface type** indicate full articles.

finch
 Darwin's finches **8**:469
 thistle **6**:371
Finless porpoise **12**:722
fins
 flying fish **6**:327
 lionfish **9**:530, 531
 marlin **9**:556
 mudskipper **10**:604
 Ocean sunfish **10**:630, 631
 pectoral **3**:191; **6**:327; **10**:604, 605, 630; **11**:699
 pelvic **6**:327
 pipefish **11**:699
 sea horse **13**:806
fir **15**:903, 915
Fire fish *See* lionfish
firefly (beetle) **5:312–313**
firefly (cave fly) **5**:312
fires **2**:71; **5**:303; **13**:802–803
fish
 angler **1:36–37**
 bony *See* bony fish
 butterfly **4**:211; **7**:398–399; **9:530–531**
 Cardinal **13**:813
 cartilaginous *See* ray; shark
 in coral reefs **4**:210–211
 Flying **6:326–327**
 Football **1**:37
 freshwater *See* freshwater fish
 grouper **4**:211
 jawless **8**:504–505
 parrot **4**:211
 saltwater *See* saltwater fish
 scorpion **4**:211
Fish crow **4**:228
fisher **12**:721
Fish hawk (osprey) **11:658–659**
fish lice **10**:631
fish owl **11**:666
flagellae **1**:25, 56, 57
flamingo **5:314–315**
Flathead catfish **3**:154–155
flea **5:316–317**; **10**:590
flicker **16**:1014, 1015
flight
 albatross **1**:22
 bat **2**:79
 dragonfly **5**:270

eagle **5**:278, 279
falcon **5**:304
flying fish **6**:326
flying lemur **6**:330
flying squirrel **6**:332
goose **6**:373
nuthatch **10**:620
Sparrow hawk **14**:854
swallow **14**:890
swan **14**:893
swift **14**:894–895
tern **15**:923
vulture **16**:969
flightless birds **5**:300–301; **8**:490–491; **11**:660–661, 686–687; **13**:774–775
Flightless scaly tailed squirrel **6**:333
Flightless wren **8**:469
Flint Ridge Mammoth Cave system **3**:159
floodplains **16**:992, 993
florets **1**:62; **4**:238; **6**:383; **14**:888–889
Florida panther **16**:993
flowering plants **1**:28–29, 46–47, 62–63; **2**:70–71, 100–101, 122–123; **3**:138–139, 156–157; **4**:212–215, 238–241; **5**:310–311; **6**:382–383; **7**:416–417, 420–421, 430–431; **9**:522–523, 546–547, 568–569; **10**:610–611; **11**:650–651, 678–679; **12**:718–719, 724–725; **13**:780–781, 786–787, 818–819; **14**:860–861, 864–865, 874–875; **16**:980–981, 998–999, 1020–1021
 carnivorous **2**:108–109; **11**:702–703; **15**:956–957
 fruits **1**:48–49; **6**:380–381; **10**:638–639; **14**:878–879; **15**:932–933
 parasitic **9**:572–573; **12**:754–755
 poisonous **6**:336–337

seeds **14**:850–851
trees **1**:16–17; **2**:96–97, 120–121; **3**:174–175, 186–187; **4**:198–199; **5**:302–303, 310–311; **7**:430–431; **9**:546–547, 552–555; **10**:624–625; **11**:670–671; **13**:788–789; **15**:912–913; **16**:1006–1007, 1020–1021
flower(s)
 Crane **2:100–101**
 of eucalypts **5**:303
 Monster **12:754–755**
 orchid **11:650–651**
 palm **11**:671
 passionflower **11:678–679**
 rose **13:786–787**
 tomato plant **15**:933
fly **5:318–319**
 crane- **4:222–223**
 tsetse **5**:318; **9**:553
Fly agaric **6**:344, 345, 347
Flycatcher plant **11**:702
flying fish **6:326–327**
flying fox **2**:78; **6:328–329**
flying lemur (colugo) **6:330–331**
flying squirrel **6:332–333**; **15**:903
foals, horse **7**:440, 441
fog **4**:249
follicles, seed **9**:547
food chains, in the ocean **10**:628
Football fish **1**:37
foraminiferans **1**:31
Forest buffalo **1**:19
forests
 deforestation **4**:211
 fires **2**:71; **5**:303
 swamp **16**:992
 See also rainforests; taiga; temperate forests
formic acid **14**:875
fossils
 coelacanth **3**:191
 dragonfly **5**:270
 scorpion **13**:800

fox **6:334–335**; **13**:827
 Arctic **15**:945
 Desert sand **4**:249
 Fennec **4**:248
 Red **4**:233; **6:334–335**; **15**:95
foxglove **6:336–337**; **13**:818; **15**:916
fox squirrel **15**:917
Free-tailed bat **2**:79
freshwater fish **2**:76–77; **3**:152–155; **11**:688–689, 700–701
freshwater habitats **8**:500–503; **16**:992
freshwater turtle **15**:948–949
frigate bird **6:338–339**; **11**:658
frog **6:340–343**; **15**:930
 tree **6**:341, 343; **11**:703
frogfish **1**:37
fruit bat **2**:79
fruit fly **5**:319
fruiting bodies **6**:345
fruits
 avocado **1:48–49**
 fig **5**:310
 follicle fruit **9**:547
 ginko **6**:363
 grapes **6:380–381**
 largest **3**:186
 lime **9:524–525**
 olive **10:638–639**
 palm **11**:671
 passionflower **11**:679
 rosehips **13**:786–787
 strawberry **14:878–879**
 tomato **15:932–933**
 true and false **14**:878, 879
fry, fish **13**:797
fungi
 fungus-alga association *See* liche
 liverwort associations with **9**:533
 and mycorrhizal associations **7**:417
fungus **1**:38, 39; **6:344–347**
fungus beetle **2**:92
fur **15**:903
 leopard **9**:519
 mink **9**:571
 mole **10**:582

Volume numbers are in **boldface type** followed by colons.
Page numbers in **boldface type** indicate full articles.

muskrat **10**:609

nutria **10**:623

otter **11**:663

seal **13**:809

wombat **16**:1012

ur seal **13**:809

izz **4**:214–215

Gaboon viper **15**:958–959

alago (bushbaby) **6:348–349**

Galah cockatoo **3**:183

allinule **4**:205; **6:350–351**

ame birds **7**:400–401;
   11:680–681, 692–693;
   12:726–727, 734–735,
   744–745; **15**:946–947

ametophytes **3**:179; **5**:307; **9**:533;
   10:592; **16**:1001

Ganges dolphin **5**:263

annet **14**:840

Garden eel **5**:288

arden squash **14**:865

arden sunflower **14**:888–889

arlic **9**:523

azelle **1**:21; **6:352–353**; **16**:1023

ecko **6:354–355**

emmae **9**:533

emsbok **11**:656, 657

ender, changing **7**:399

entoo penguin **11**:686

eoffroy's long-nosed bat **2**:100

eographic terrapin **15**:924

erbil **4**:249; **6:356–357**; **8**:459

erenuk **6**:352

estation periods **11**:697

iant anteater **1**:40–41

iant armadillo **1**:44

iant bandicoot **7**:407

iant bustard **2**:126, 127

iant Caribbean sea anemone
   13:804

iant clam **3**:176, 177; **10**:629

iant cowbird **11**:655

iant desert hairy scorpion **13**:800,
   801

iant eland **5**:291

iant fluted clam **3**:176

iant forest hog **16**:976

iant (Great) gerbil **6**:356, 357

Giant granadilla **11**:679

Giant gum tree **5**:302

Giant hummingbird **7**:446

Giant kelp **8**:482, 483; **10**:628

Giant Maori wrasse **16**:1017

Giant marine toad **15**:931

Giant millipede **9**:566

Giant otter **11**:662

Giant panda **1**:63; **2**:82, 83;
   11:672–673

Giant pangolin **11**:675

Giant puffball **6**:346, 347

Giant salamander **13**:794

Giant scops owl **11**:667

Giant sea bass **2**:77

Giant sequoia **13**:816, 817

Giant silkworm moth (*Saturniidae*)
   10:594, 596–597

Giant skua **14**:840, 841

Giant spider crab **4**:218

Giant squid **14**:867

giant tortoise **15**:935

gibbon **6:358–359**

Gila monster **6:360–361**

gills, axolotl **1**:52, 53

ginkgo (Maidenhair tree)
   6:362–363

giraffe **6:364–365**; **10**:637

Glacier bear **2**:84

glass eels **5**:289

glass frog **6**:341–342

Glaucous macaw **9**:545

global warming **12**:759

glochids **3**:138

Glossy ibis **8**:462

gnetophyte **6:366–367;**
   16:988–989

gnu *See* wildebeest

goat antelopes **10**:606–607

goat(s) **6:368–369**; **10**:599
   See also chamois; ibex

Gobi Desert **4**:249

golden-brown algae **1**:25

Golden eagle **5**:278, 279, 280,
   281; **13**:793

Golden hamster **7**:410, 411

Golden-headed tamarin **15**:904

Golden jackal **8**:472, 473

Golden lion tamarin **15**:904, 905

Golden pheasant **11**:692

Golden-rumped elephant shrew
   5:296–297

Golden-shouldered parrot **11**:677

goldfinch **6:370–371**

goldfish **3**:153

Goliath beetle **2**:92

Goliath bird-eating spider **15**:909

Goliath frog **6**:340

Goliath heron **7**:424

golomyanka **8**:501

goosander (Common merganser)
   9:564, 565

goose **6:372–375**

goosefish **1**:36

goosegrass **3**:175

Gooseneck barnacle **15**:927

gopher tortoise **15**:934–935

gorgets **7**:447

Gorgonian fan coral **4**:209

gorgonin **4**:206

gorilla **6:376–377**; **12**:759

goshawk **7**:415

Gould's (Sand) monitor **10**:586,
   587

gourd **14**:864–865

grackle **6:378–379**

grains, wheat **16**:998

grape **6:380–381**

grapefruit **9**:524

Grape phylloxera **6**:381

grapevine **6**:380

grass **6:382–383**
   and grasslands **7**:393
   and horses **7**:440
   Pampas **6**:382, 383
   See also bamboo; rice;
      sugarcane; wheat

grasshopper **7:390–391**

grassland **7:392–393**
   birds **2**:126–127; **7**:393

Gray catbird **9**:574

Gray cockatiel **3**:182

Gray-headed chickadee **3**:167

Gray-headed flying fox **6**:329

Gray heron **16**:991

Gray jay **2**:113

Gray (Common) moorhen **6**:351

Gray (Common) rhea **13**:774, 775

Gray squirrel **15**:916

Gray wolf **15**:903, 945; **16**:1008,
   1009, 1010, 1011

great apes **11**:648

Great barracuda **2**:74, 75

Great Barrier Reef **4**:210, 211;
   13:805

Great black cockatoo **3**:182

Great blue heron **7**:424, 425

Great bustard **2**:127

Great clam **3**:176

Greater black-backed gull **7**:404

Greater flamingo **5**:314, 315

Greater (Thick-tailed) galago **6**:349

Greater hedgehog tenrec **15**:918

Greater honeyguide **7**:432–433

Greater prairie chicken **12**:726–727

Greater (Common) rhea **13**:774,
   775

Greater roadrunner **13**:782, 783

Greater yellowleg **13**:791

Great (Giant) gerbil **6**:356, 357

Great gray owl **11**:664–665, 666;
   15:915

Great gray slug **14**:847

Great green bush cricket **4**:224

Great hornbill **7**:434

Great horned owl **4**:229; **11**:665,
   667; **14**:843

Great Indian bustard **2**:126, 127

Great northern diver **9**:539

Great pipefish **11**:698–699

Great plains toad **15**:931

Great skua **14**:841

Great-tailed grackle **6**:379

Great white shark **4**:211; **13**:820,
   821, 822

grebe **7:394–395**; **11**:665; **16**:993

green algae **1**:24–25

Green anaconda **1**:32

Green-cheeked Amazon parrot
   11:676

greenhouse effect **12**:759

Green kingfisher **8**:488

Volume numbers are in **boldface type** followed by colons.
Page numbers in **boldface type** indicate full articles.

Greenland collared (Collared) lemming 8:508, 509

Greenland halibut 7:409

Green oropendola 11:655

Green tree python 12:743

Green turtle 15:950, 951

Green-winged (Red-and-green) macaw 9:544, 545

Grevy's zebra 16:1022, 1023

Grizzly bear 2:82, 83–84; 5:298

grosbeak 3:148

groundhog 7:396–397; 15:917

ground pine 3:178, 179

ground squirrel 4:248; 12:728
    Arctic 15:945

groundwater 16:990–991

grouper 4:211; 7:398–399

grouse 7:400–401, 417
    Red 7:417

guanaco 3:145; 9:534, 535

guard hairs 2:86; 10:606, 609; 13:809

Guinea baboon 1:54

Guinea Forest red colobus monkey 4:200

guinea pig 7:402–403

Gulf of California porpoise 12:723

gull 4:233; 7:404–405; 12:738; 13:813; 14:840

Gunn's bandicoot 7:406–407

gymnosperms 4:236; 6:362–363, 366, 367
    See also conifers; cycad; ginko; gnetophyte

Gyr falcon 5:304

H

habitats (and biomes)
    cave 3:158–159
    coral reef 4:210–211
    cultivated land 4:232–233
    desert 4:246–249
    grassland 7:392–393
    island 8:468–469
    lake, river, and estuary 8:500–503
    mountain 10:598–599
    ocean 10:626–627
    polar regions 12:716–717
    rainforest 12:756–759
    scrubland 13:802–803
    suburban 14:882–883
    taiga 15:902–903
    temperate forest 15:914–917
    tide pool and coast 15:926–927
    tundra 15:944–945
    urban 15:954–955
    wetland 3:157; 9:527; 12:749; 16:990–993

haddock 3:188

hagfish 8:504

hairs, guard 2:86; 10:606, 609; 13:809

Hairy-footed gerbil 6:356

hairy-nosed wombat 16:1012

Hairy stone crab 4:218

hake 3:188

halibut 7:408–409

hallucinogens 6:347

halteres 4:222

halvah 13:819

hamadryad (King cobra) 3:180, 181

Hamadryas baboon 1:54, 55

hamster 7:410–411

Harbor porpoise 12:722, 723

hare 7:412–413; 12:750–751
    Arctic or Mountain 7:412–413; 15:945
    Patagonian 7:403
    Snowshoe 9:542

harems
    baboon 1:55
    horse 7:440
    saiga 13:793
    sambar 13:799
    sea lion 13:811
    tree kangaroo 15:939
    zebra 16:1022, 1023

hare and rabbit family 7:412–413; 12:750–751

Harlequin bass 2:77

Harp seal 12:714; 13:808

Harpy eagle 5:279–280

Harrier hawk 7:414–415

Harvester termite 15:921

Harvest mouse 4:233; 10:600

Hawaiian goose 6:375

Hawaiian islands 8:468

hawk 7:414–415
    Sparrow 8:484, 485; 14:854–855

hawker dragonfly 5:270, 271

hawk moth 10:594, 594–596

Hawksbill turtle 15:950, 951

hawthorn 15:915

hazel 2:96; 15:915

headless invertebrates See invertebrates, headless

heart urchin 13:813

heath 13:802

heather 7:416–417

heaths 7:417

hedgehog 7:418–419; 15:917

hellbender 13:794, 795

hemlock (coniferous tree) 7:421; 15:915

hemlock, Poison (flowering plant) 7:420–421

hemp 14:874

henbane 4:241

Henley's (pygmy) gerbil 6:356

herbaceous plants 11:650, 678

herbivores, suburban 14:883

herbs 7:420
    forest 15:916
    scrubland 13:802

hermaphrodites 5:283
    sequential 7:399

hermit crab 7:422–423; 13:805

Hermit crab anemone 13:805

heroin 12:719

heron 7:424–425; 16:993
    Gray 16:991

herring 7:426–427

Herring gull 7:404–405

hibernation 15:917
    axolotl 1:53
    bat 2:81
    dormouse 5:267; 15:917
    groundhog 7:397
    hedgehog 7:419

ladybug 8:499

poorwill 14:895

rattlesnake 12:763
    See also aestivation

hickorie 15:915

Hill myna 14:873

Himalayan pine 11:695

Himalayan poppy 12:718

Himalayan tahr 6:369

hippopotamus 7:428–429

Hoary bat 2:78

hog-nosed skunk 14:842

hold-fast 8:482

holly 7:430–431
    Desert 4:249

Holly blue butterfly 7:431

Honey badger 1:60, 61; 7:432–433; 14:863

honeybee 2:88–89; 6:337

honeyeater 2:70, 71

honeyguide 1:61; 7:432–433

honeysuckle (a banksia) 2:70–71

honeysuckle, Jamaican (a passionflower) 11:679

Hooded (Indian) cobra 3:180, 181

Hooded crow 4:229

Hooded merganser 9:564, 565

Hooded seal 12:714

Hooded skunk 14:842

hoofed mammals 1:14–15, 18–19, 42–43; 2:94–95, 104–105, 124–125; 3:142–145, 150–151, 162–163; 4:242–245, 252–25; 5:264–265, 290–295, 298–29; 6:352–353, 364–365, 368–36; 7:428–429, 438–441; 8:458–461, 466–467; 9:534–535; 10:588–589, 606–607, 616–617, 636–637; 11:656–657, 682–683; 13:776–779, 792–793; 14:862–863; 15:906–907; 16:976–977, 1004–1005, 1018–1019, 1022–1023

hooves, chamois 3:162

hornbeam 2:96

hornbill(s) 7:434–435

horned owl 11:666
    Great 4:229; 11:665, 667; 14:843

Volume numbers are in **boldface type** followed by colons. Page numbers in **boldface type** indicate full articles.

orned puffin 12:738
rnet 7:436–437
rns
  African buffalo 1:18
  chamois 3:163
  eland 5:290–291
  gazelle 6:353
  goat 6:369
  Musk ox 10:606, 607
  oryx 11:657
  pronghorn 1:43
  rhinoceros 13:776, 778, 779
  sheep 2:94–95
  yak 16:1019
rnworms 4:233; 10:594–595
rse 7:438–441
rsefly 5:319
rseshoe (King) crab 7:442–443
rse's hoof clam 3:176
rsetail 7:444–445
oubara 2:126–127
ouse cricket 4:225
ousefly 5:318
ouse martin 14:883
ouse mouse 10:600–601
ouse sparrow 13:785;
  14:852–853
ouston toad 15:931
ver fly 5:319
uanstan Chico, Mount 10:598
uemul 4:245
uman flea 5:317
umble (or Sensitive) plant
  9:568–569
mmingbird 7:446–447
umpback whale 16:994,
  995–996
umphead wrasse 16:1017
acinth 14:860
yacinth macaw 9:544
brids, plant 9:525; 14:878–879
dra 8:454–455
drogen sulfide 10:627
dromedusans 7:423
drophobia 6:335
drothermal vents 10:627–628,
  629
ena 8:456–457; 13:777; 16:1005
phae 6:344; 7:416
rax 8:458–459

I
ibex 8:460–461
ibis 8:462–463; 16:993
Iceland poppy 12:718
ichneumon wasp 16:978–979
iguana 8:464–465
impala 1:21; 8:466–467; 16:1023
Imperial woodpecker 16:1015
incisors 3:147
  musk deer 4:245
Indian cobra 3:180, 181
Indian (Asian) elephant 5:294,
  295
Indian flying fox 6:328, 329
Indian gray mongoose 10:584–585
Indian Ocean 10:626, 627
Indian pangolin 11:675
Indian (Common) peacock 11:680,
  681
Indian red-footed gerbil 6:356
Indian rhinoceros 13:776, 778
Indian turnip (jack-in-the pulpit)
  1:46–47
Indian wild donkey 5:264
Indian wolf 16:1011
Indigo macaw 9:545
inflorescences 2:70, 100; 3:156,
  186–187; 4:213
ink 10:635
  squid 14:867
insect eaters 7:418–419;
  10:582–583; 11:674–675;
  13:826–827; 15:918–919
  relations 1:40–41, 44–45;
    14:844–845
insecticides 4:233
insects 1:38–39; 15:920–921;
  16:970–971
  social 1:38–39; 15:920–921
  suburban 14:882
  winged 2:88–89, 92–93;
    3:134–137, 140–141,
    172–173, 184–185;
    4:222–225; 5:270–271,
    284–285, 312–313,
    318–319; 7:390–391,

436–437; 8:498–499;
    10:590–591, 594–597;
    12:730–731; 14:838–839;
    16:978–979
  wingless 5:316–317
invertebrates, headless 4:206–209;
  8:454–455, 476–477;
  13:804–805
iodine 8:483
Irish moss 15:926
Irish Potato Famine 12:725
ironbark 5:302
island 8:468–469
ivory 5:294, 295
Ivory-billed woodpecker 16:1015

J
jacana 8:470–471
jackal 8:472–473; 14:863;
  16:1005
jack-in-the-pulpit 1:46–47
jackrabbit (hare) 12:750–751
jaeger 14:840
jaguar 1:41, 44; 8:474–475;
  10:623; 15:907
Jamaican crow 4:228
Jamaican honeysuckle 11:679
Japanese crested ibis 8:463
Japanese dormouse 5:267
Japanese flying squirrel 6:332
Japanese larch 8:507
Japanese white pine 2:116
Javan rhinoceros 13:778
jawless fish 8:504–505
jaws, snake 1:33; 12:743
jay 14:854; 15:916
  Blue 2:112–113
jellyfish 8:476–477; 10:630
jerboa 10:600
jewfish 7:399
jimsonweed 4:241; 15:932
joey 8:479
Joshua tree 16:1020, 1021
jumping mouse 10:600, 603
jumping spider 10:599; 14:857,
  858

K
kakapo 8:469
Kamloops trout 15:940
kangaroo 8:478–479
  tree 15:938–939
kangaroo mouse 13:830
kangaroo rat 4:248; 8:480–481;
  10:600; 13:803
karri 5:302
katydid 4:225
kelp 8:482–483; 10:626, 628;
  15:927
Kelp pipefish 11:699
kelt 13:797
Kermodes bear 2:84
kestrel 8:484–485; 14:883
  American (Sparrow hawk)
    8:484, 485; 14:854–855
Keyhole urchin 13:813
keys (seeds), of maples 9:555
killdeer 8:486–487
Killer whale 5:263; 11:687;
  16:996, 997
King cobra 3:180, 181
King (Horseshoe) crab 7:442–443
kingfisher 8:488–489
  bee-eater 2:90–91
kingfisher family 8:488–489,
  496–497
Kirk's dik-dik 4:252, 253
kite 16:993
Kitti's hog-nosed bat 2:79
kiwi 8:469, 490–491
koala 5:302; 8:492–493; 13:803
Kodiak bear 2:82
Koi carp 3:153
Komodo dragon 8:469, 494–495;
  10:586
kookaburra 8:489, 496–497
Korean gray rat 7:411
Kori bustard 2:126, 127
krill 10:627, 628–629; 13:829;
  16:996
Kuhl gecko 6:355

L
lactic acid 1:59
ladybug 8:498–499; 14:882
lagomorphs 7:412
lake 8:500–502; 16:992

Volume numbers are in **boldface type** followed by colons.
Page numbers in **boldface type** indicate full articles.

Lake sturgeon 14:880–881

lampblack 11:695

lamprey 8:504–505

Langur monkey 4:243

lanternfish 10:629

lanugo 13:808

Lapland bunting 12:716

larch 8:506–507; 10:598; 15:902–903; 16:991

Larch sawfly 8:507

Largemouth bass 2:76–77

larvae
  bee 2:88
  beetle 2:93; 16:978
  caddis fly 3:140–141
  cicada 3:173
  coral 4:209
  crab 4:219
  crane fly 4:222, 223
  eel 5:288–289
  firefly 5:313
  flea 5:317
  fly (maggots) 5:318
  hornet 7:437
  jellyfish 8:477
  ladybug 8:499
  lamprey 8:505
  lobster 9:537
  mosquito 10:590
  sea anemone 13:805
  wasp 16:979
  See also axolotl; caterpillars; nymphs

laryngeal pouches 11:648

late blight 12:725

lateral line 13:822

latex 5:310; 12:719; 13:788–789

Laughing kookaburra (Laughing jackass) 8:489, 496, 497

laurel 13:803

Laurel bay (Southern magnolia) 9:546, 547

laver 8:483

leaf-cutting ant 1:38, 39; 6:346, 347

Least chipmunk 3:171

Least pygmy owl 11:666

Least weasel 16:984–985

Leatherback turtle 15:948, 950

Leather carp 3:153

leatherjackets 4:222, 223

leatherleaf 16:991

leaves 2:100
  desert plant 4:247, 249
  of grasses 6:383
  hairs 2:71
  largest 11:670
  pine 11:694
  scale-like 6:367
  sensitive to touch 9:568–569; 15:956–957
  tea 15:912, 913
  variegated 7:431
  See also tendrils

Ledger bark 3:175

legs, double-jointed 7:414–415

legumes 1:16; 14:850

leks (display grounds) 12:726, 727; 13:790, 791

lemming 8:508–509; 15:945

lemon 9:524–525

Lemon shark 13:822

lemur 8:510–511

leopard 1:15; 9:518–519; 16:1005
  differs from the jaguar 8:474
  Snow 9:519; 10:599

Leopard moray eel 4:211; 5:288, 289

Leopard seal 11:687; 12:717; 13:808

Lesser bladderwort 2:108

Lesser fairy armadillo 1:44

Lesser galago 6:348, 349

Lesser hedgehog tenrec 15:918, 919

Lesser honeyguide 7:433

Lesser long-nosed bat 3:139

Lesser (Red) panda 11:672, 673

Lesser prairie chicken 12:726, 727

Lesser roadrunner 13:783

Lesser yellowleg 13:791

leverets 7:413

liana 6:367

Liberian coffee 4:198

Liberian mongoose 10:585

lice, fish 10:631

lichen 1:25; 6:347; 9:520–521; 10:598; 12:717; 15:902, 926

lightning bug (firefly) 5:312–313

lily 9:522–523
  See also spider plant

Lily of the field 9:523

Lily of the valley 9:523

lime 9:524–525

limequat 9:525

limpet 15:926

limpkin 9:526–527

ling (heather) 3:188; 7:416–417

lint 4:214–215

lion 1:15; 9:518–519, 528–529; 13:777; 16:977, 1005, 1008
  Mountain (puma) 1:41, 44; 12:721, 740–741; 15:907

lionfish 1:35; 4:211; 9:530–531

Lion-tailed macaque 2:72

lion tamarin 15:904

Little blue (Spix's) macaw 9:545

Little curlew 4:235

Little spotted kiwi 8:491

liverwort 9:532–533

living fossil 6:362

lizard(s) 3:160–161; 6:354–355, 360–361; 8:464–465, 494–495; 10:586–587
  Eastern fence 8:465
  Texas horned 8:465

llama 3:145; 9:534–535; 10:599

Loblolly pine 11:695

lobster 9:536–537

locust 7:390, 391

Long-billed curlew 4:234–235

Longfin squid 14:866

Long-leaf pine 11:695

Long-nosed bandicoot 7:407

Long-nosed echidna 5:287

Long-tailed pangolin 11:675

Long-tailed weasel 16:984, 985

Long-tongued bat 2:79

loofah 14:864

loon 9:538–539

lorikeet 2:71

Louisiana quillwort 12:748, 749

Lumholtz's tree kangaroo 15:938, 939

Luminous moss 10:593

Luna moth 10:596

lungfish 9:540–541; 13:824

lygus bug 4:215

lynx 2:115; 9:519, 542–543; 15:903

M

Macadamia nut 2:70

macaque 2:72
  Barbary (Barbary ape) 2:72–73

macaw 9:544–545; 12:757, 758

mackerel 15:942

Macleay's specter 16:971

McMahon's viper 13:831

macrotermes 15:921

madder 3:175

Madonna lily 9:523

maggots 5:318

Magnificent frigate bird 6:339

magnolia 9:546–547; 15:915

magpie 2:113

mahogany 12:758

Maidenhair fern 5:306

Maidenhair tree (ginkgo) 6:362–363

maize (corn) 4:212–213; 6:346

Malacite sunbird 14:887

malaria 3:174; 5:318; 10:590, 59

Malarial mosquito 10:591

Malayan flying lemur 6:330

Malayan pangolin 11:675

Malayan tapir 15:906

Malaysian wood nymph 16:971

mallard 5:273, 274

mallow, Desert 4:247

mammals 4:248
  egg-laying 5:286–287; 12:710–711
  hoofed See hoofed mammals
  sea See sea mammals
  temperate forest 15:917

mammary glands, in egg-laying mammals 5:287; 12:711

mammoth 5:292

manatee 9:548–549

Mandarin duck 5:272–273

mandrill 9:550–551

Volume numbers are in **boldface type** followed by colons. Page numbers in **boldface type** indicate full articles.

See also baboon
manfish **3**:159
mangrove **4**:210; **9:552–553;** **10**:605; **16**:991
    Red (American) **9**:552–553; **16**:992
mangrove swamps **10**:604; **16**:991
Manitoba maple **10**:597
Many-rayed star **14**:870
maple **9:554–555**
maple syrup **9**:555
Map terrapin **15**:924
maquis **13**:803
Marabou stork **14**:877; **16**:969
Marbled gecko **6**:355
Margay cat **10**:632, 633
marigold **14**:888
    Corn **4**:233
Marine iguana **8**:464, 465
Maritime pine **11**:695
Markham's storm petrel **11**:690
marlin **9:556–557**
marmoset **9:558–559; 15**:904
marshes **9**:527; **16**:991, 992
    cattail **3**:157
Marsh hawk **7**:414, 415
Marsupial mole **9:560–561**
marsupials **7**:406–407; **8**:478–479, 492–493; **9**:560–561; **10**:618–619; **11**:646–647; **15**:910–911, 938–939; **16**:972–973, 1012–1013
martin **4**:233; **14**:891
Mat-forming quillwort **12**:749
maypop **11**:679
Meadow jumping mouse **10**:602, 603
meadow vole **16**:967
medicines and drugs **4**:241; **6**:336, 337, 347, 363, 367; **12**:719, 757; **16**:1006
Meeoioing frog **6**:341
meerkat **9:562–563; 10**:585
melon (for echolocation) **5**:263; **16**:996
merganser **9:564–565**
meristems **6**:383
merlin **5**:305
Merriam's kangaroo rat **8**:480, 481
mesquite **4**:247; **9**:573

metabolism **4**:248
metamorphosis **1**:52, 53; **15**:930
    complete **3**:135, 140
    degenerative **1**:37
    incomplete **3**:173
methane bacteria **1**:59
Mexican bee **11**:651
Mexican burrowing python **12**:742
Mexican poppy **12**:719
Mexican pygmy salamander **13**:794
Mexican red knee **15**:909
Mexican vanilla **11**:650, 651
Mexican vole **16**:967
Mexican wolf **16**:1011
Middle Eastern scorpion **13**:800
midwife toad **15**:931
migration
    bird **2**:111, 127; **4**:221, 230, 231, 235; **5**:274; **6**:373, 375; **7**:425; **9**:564; **10**:613; **11**:659; **13**:784, 785; **14**:855, 890, 891, 895; **15**:922–923
    butterfly **3**:136
    caribou **3**:151
    crab **4**:218
    eel **5**:288–289
    Horseshoe crab **7**:443
    lemming **8**:509
    lobster **9**:537
    salmon **13**:796–797
    trout **15**:941
    tuna **15**:943
    whale **16**:994
milk, crop **5**:268, 315
millipede **9:566–567**
Mimic blenny **16**:1016
mimicry **4**:225
    by butterflies **3**:137
    by parrots **11**:677
mimosa **1**:16; **9:568–569**
Mindanao moonrat **7**:419
mink **9:570–571**
Minke whale **16**:997
mint **13**:803
Mirror carp **3**:153

Mississippi cat **3**:154
mistletoe **9:572–573**
Mitchell's water monitor **10**:586–587
mockingbird **9:574–575**
molars **11**:672
molasses **14**:885
mold **6**:344
mole **10:582–583**
    African golden **4**:249
    Mole cricket **4**:225
mole salamander **1**:52
mollusks **10**:634–635; **14**:846–849, 866–867
    bivalve **3**:176–177
    molts **7**:412; **16**:970, 985
    feathers **5**:272
Monarch birch **2**:97
Monarch butterfly **3**:136, 137
Mongolian gerbil **6**:356, 357
mongoose **10:584–585**
mongoose family **9**:562–563; **10**:584–585
Monito gecko **6**:355
monitor **10:586–587**
    Komodo dragon **8:494–495**
Monkey-eating eagle **5**:279–280
monkey(s) **1**:54–55; **2**:72–73; **9**:550–551, 558–559; **10**:614–615; **12**:732–733; **15**:904–905, 952–953
    colobus **4:200–201; 12**:732
    Langur **4**:243
    Night (Owl) **10:614–615**
monocotyledons **6**:383; **9**:522
monoculture **4**:232
monogamy **10**:615
Monster flower (rafflesia) **12:754–755**
Montezuma's oropendola **11**:655
moonrat **7**:419
moorhen (Common gallinule) **4**:205; **6**:350
moose **10:588–589; 15**:903; **16**:1010
morphine **12**:719

mosquito **3**:174; **5**:318, 319; **10:590–591; 11**:703
moss **10:592–593; 12**:717; **15**:944–945
Mother spleenwort **5**:307
moth(s) **3**:134, 135; **10:594–597**
    Owlett **4**:215
    silkworm (*Bombycidae*) **10**:596; **14:838–839**
    and sloths **14**:845
    and spiders **14**:858
    Tobacco hawk **4**:233; **10**:594–596
    yucca **16**:1020–1021
mountain **10:598–599**
Mountain ash (Giant gum tree) **5**:302
Mountain bluebird **2**:110, 111
Mountain buttercup **10**:599
Mountain chickadee **3**:167
Mountain goat **6**:368, 369
Mountain gorilla **6**:376
Mountain (Arctic) hare **7**:412–413
Mountain lilac **13**:803
Mountain lion (puma) **1**:41, 44; **12**:721, **740–741; 15**:907
Mountain tapir **15**:906
Mountain toucan **15**:937
Mountain zebra **16**:1022–1023
Mourning dove **5**:269
mouse **10:600–603; 14**:883
    Harvest **4**:233; **10**:600
    pocket **4**:248
Mouse bandicoot **7**:407
Mouse lemur **8**:510, 511
mud bath **15**:906
Mud chicken **6**:350, 351
mudpuppy **1**:52; **13**:795
mudskipper **10:604–605**
mud turtle **15**:949–950
mulberry **14**:839, 874
Mule deer **12**:741
muntjac **4**:244
Muscadine grape **6**:380
mushroom **6**:344, 346
musk **4**:245; **13**:827
musk deer **4**:245
Musk ox **10:606–607; 15**:945
muskrat **1**:27; **3**:157; **10:608–609; 16**:991

Volume numbers are in **boldface type** followed by colons.
Page numbers in **boldface type** indicate full articles.

musk turtle **15**:948, 949

musquash **10**:609

mustang **7**:438

mustard **10:610–611**

Mute swan **14**:892

mycelia **6**:344, 345

mycorrhizae **6**:347; **7**:417

myna bird **14**:872, 873

myriapods **9**:566–567

myrosin **10**:611

myrtle **13**:803

N

nailtail wallaby **16**:972–973

Namib Desert **4**:246, 249; **16**:988

narwhal **16**:994

Natterer's (Red) piranha **11**:700

nectar **1**:17; **2**:89

Needle-clawed galago **6**:349

Needle palm **11**:670–671

nematocysts **13**:805

nematodes **6**:345–346

Neon tetra **11**:701

neotony **13**:795

Net-throwing spider **14**:858

New Guinean Buff-faced pygmy
   parrot **11**:677

New Holland honeyeater **2**:70

nightingale **10:612–613**

Nightingale monkey **15**:905

Night monkey **10:614–615**

nightshade

   Common or Black **4**:241

   Deadly (belladonna) **4:240–241**;
      12:724; **15**:932

Nile crocodile **4**:226, 227

Nile monitor **10**:586–587

Nile River **8**:500, 503

nilgai **10:616–617**

Nilgiri tahr **6**:369

Nine-banded armadillo **1**:44–45

nocturnal animals

   aardvark **1**:14

   armadillo **1**:44

   badger **1**:60, 61

   bat **2**:78; **6**:329

   flying lemur **6**:330

   flying squirrel **6**:333

   gerbil **6**:357

   hedgehog **7**:418

lynx **9**:542

Night monkey **10**:614, 615

   pine marten **11**:696–697

   raccoon **12**:752

   in the rainforest **12**:757

   sambar **13**:798

   skunk **14**:843

   tenrec **15**:918

   tiger **15**:928

   walking stick **16**:970

   wombat **16**:1013

North African elephant shrew
   5:297

North American black bear **2**:82

North American (West Indian)
   manatee **9**:548, 549

North American mistletoe **9**:573

North American mountain goat
   6:368

North American porcupine **12**:721

North American (Common)
   raccoon **12**:752, 753; **15**:955

North American river otter **11**:662

North Atlantic giant violet jellyfish
   8:477

North Atlantic (American) lobster
   9:536, 537

Northern bald ibis **8**:463

Northern bobwhite **12**:744

Northern cardinal **3**:148–149;
   14:883

Northern elephant seal **13**:808,
   809

Northern flying squirrel **6**:332;
   15:903

Northern jacana **8**:470, 471

Northern mockingbird **9**:574, 575

Northern oriole **11**:652–653

Northern pike **8**:501–502

Northern red salamander **13**:794

Northern tamandua **1**:40, 41

Northwestern crow **4**:228

Norway lemming **8**:508, 509

Norway maple **9**:554

Norway rat *See* Brown rat

Nubian wild donkey **5**:264

nudibranch (sea slug) **14**:871

numbat **10:618–619**

nuthatch **10:620–621; 15**:917

nutria **10:622–623**

nuts **2**:120

   paradise **2**:120

nymphs, dragonfly **5**:271

O

oak **10:624–625; 15**:915

ocean **10:626–629**

Ocean sunfish **10:630–631**

ocelot **10:632–633**

Ocoee salamander **13**:794

octopus **10:634–635**

oil

   olive **10**:639

   pollution **10**:629; **11**:663

   poppy seed **12**:719

   sesame **13**:819

   soy **14**:851

   sunflower **14**:889

oilbird **3**:159

okapi **10:636–637**

Okeechobee, Lake **9**:527;
   16:992–993

Okefenokee Swamp **9**:527

olive **10:638–639; 13**:803

Olive baboon **1**:54

Olive colobus **4**:201

olive oil **10**:639

onion **9**:523; **14**:860

opium **12**:719

Opium poppy **12**:718, 719

opossum **11:646–647; 14**:883;
   15:955

orange **9**:524

orangutan **11:648–649**

orca (Killer whale) **5**:263; **11**:687;
   16:996, 997

orchid **11:650–651**

Ord kangaroo rat **8**:481

Oriental white stork **14**:877

Orinoco hog (capybara) **3:146–147**

oriole **11:652–653**

Ornate wobbegong **13**:822

oropendola **6**:379; **11:654–655**

oryx **11:656–657**

osprey **11:658–659**

ostrich **7**:393; **11:660–661**

Ostrich fern **5**:307

otter **11:662–663**

   Sea **11**:662–663; **13**:813

ounce (Snow leopard) **9**:519;
   10:599

ovipositors **4**:223; **5**:310;
   16:978–979

owl **4**:233; **11:664–667; 15**:917;
   16:1015

   Great horned **4**:229; **11**:665,
      667; **14**:843

Owlett moth **4**:215

Owl (Night) monkey **10:614–615**

oxpecker **11:668–669; 14**:872

P

Pacific barracuda **2**:74

Pacific herring **7**:426

Pacific loon **9**:538

Pacific Ocean **10**:626–627

Pacific salmon **8**:502; **13**:796

Pacific sea horse **13**:806

pack rat **12**:761

Painted bunting **14**:852

Painted hunting dog *See* African
   wild dog

Painted terrapin **15**:949

Painted turtle **15**:948, 949

Pale-throated three-toed sloth
   14:844, 845

palm **11:670–671**

   Coconut **3:186–187; 11**:671

Palm cockatoo **3**:182

Palm crow **4**:228

pampas **7**:392

Pampas grass **6**:382, 383

panda **11:672–673**

   Giant **1**:63; **2**:82, 83;
      11:672–673

pangolin **1**:40; **11:674–675**

panther **9**:519

   Florida **16**:993

Paper birch **2**:96; **15**:916

paramo **7**:392

parasites

   amoebae **1**:31

Volume numbers are in **boldface type** followed by colons.
Page numbers in **boldface type** indicate full articles.

angler fish **1**:37
flowering plants *See* flowering
    plants, parasitic
lampreys **8**:504
malarial **3**:174–175; **10**:591
oxpecker **11**:668–669
Trypanosoma **9**:553
arasitoids **16**:979
arma wallaby **16**:973
arrot **11**:676–677
arrot family **3**:182–183;
    9:544–545; **11**:676–677
arrotfish **1**:35; **4**:208, 211
arsley, Cow **7**:421
assenger pigeon **5**:269
assionflower **11**:678–679
assion vine **11**:679
atagium **6**:332
atagonian hare **7**:403
each **13**:786
eacock **11**:680–681
ea crab **4**:218
ear **13**:786
eat **16**:991
eatlands **10**:592
eat moss **10**:593
eccary **11**:682–683
elican **11**:684–685; **16**:991
en (swan) **14**:893
en, of squid **14**:866–867
enguin **11**:686–687; **12**:716, 717
enicillin **6**:347
ennant's red colobus monkey
    4:201
erch **11**:688–689
erching birds **2**:98–99, 102–103,
    110–113, 118–119; **3**:148–149,
    166–167; **4**:228–229;
    6:370–371, 378–379;
    9:574–575; **10**:612–613,
    620–621; **11**:652–655,
    668–669; **12**:764–765;
    13:784–785; **14**:852–853,
    872–873, 886–887, 890–891;
    16:986–987
ère David's deer **4**:244
eregrine falcon **5**:304, 305;
    15:954–955
erennial plants **4**:240; **6**:336;
    12:724

desert **4**:247
    grasses **6**:382
    high-altitude **10**:599
    perfumes **13**:787
Peringuey's desert adder **13**:831
periwinkle **15**:926
permafrost **15**:944
pesticides **5**:281, 305; **11**:659,
    669; **14**:891
pests, grasshoppers as **7**:391
petrel **11**:690–691; **12**:716–717;
    14:841
pheasant **4**:233; **11**:692–693
pheasant family **11**:680–681,
    692–693; **12**:734–735,
    744–745
pheromones **9**:559
    butterfly **3**:137
    caddis fly **3**:140
    moth **10**:596
    walking stick **16**:971
Philippine falconet **5**:304
photosynthesis **10**:627
Pied-billed grebe **7**:395
pigeon **5**:268, 269
piglets **16**:976–977
pigments, from lichens **9**:521
pike, Northern **8**:501–502
Pileated woodpecker
    16:1014–1015
pinaster **11**:695
pine **10**:598; **11**:694–695; **15**:915
    Japanese white **2**:116
pineapple **2**:122, 123
pineapple family **9**:553
pine marten **11**:696–697
Pink bollworm **4**:215
Pink cockatoo **3**:183
Pink fairy armadillo **1**:44
pipefish **11**:698–699
piranha **11**:700–701
pitcher plant **11**:702–703
pit viper **15**:959
Plains buffalo **2**:124–115
Plains (Common) zebra
    16:1022–1023

plankton **4**:209; **7**:427; **10**:628
plantlets **5**:307; **14**:860, 861
plants
    flowering *See* flowering plants
    simple (algae) **1**:24–25
    without roots or leaves
        9:532–533; **10**:592–593
Plasmodium **10**:591
plastron **15**:925, 934, 949
platypus **12**:710–711
plover, killdeer **8**:486–487
plum **13**:786
pocket gopher **12**:712–713;
    13:830
pocket mouse **4**:248; **13**:803
pods (whale) **16**:997
poison
    affecting birds **4**:203; **5**:281
    protoctist algal **1**:25
    stinging nettle **14**:875
    tomato plant **15**:932
    See also venom
Poison black cherry *See* Deadly
    nightshade
Poison hemlock **7**:420–421
poisonous plants **4**:240–241;
    15:932
Polar bear **2**:82, 83; **12**:714–715,
    717; **16**:1008
polar regions **12**:716–717
Polar willow **12**:716
pollen **2**:89
    orchid **11**:651
pollination
    by animals **2**:71
    by birds **1**:29; **2**:71, 100, 101
    by insects **1**:47; **5**:310–311;
        12:718, 755; **16**:981,
        1020–1021
    cross- **6**:380
    of orchids **11**:651
    self- **6**:380
    wind- **2**:97; **4**:213; **6**:383;
        14:875; **16**:998
pollinia **11**:651
pollock (pollack) **3**:189

pollution
    freshwater **8**:503
    marine **10**:629; **11**:663, 687;
        15:927
polyps **4**:206, 207, 208, 210
ponds **8**:500, 502; **16**:992
Pond turtle **15**:949
poplar **16**:1007
poppy **12**:718–719
    Corn **4**:233
porcupine **12**:720–721
porcupine fish **12**:737
porcupine wood **3**:187
porpoise **12**:722–723; **16**:994
Portuguese man-of-war **8**:454, 476
potato **4**:241; **12**:724–725
pouch
    of marsupials **5**:286, 287;
        11:647; **15**:911; **16**:972,
        973, 1012
    sea horse **13**:806–807
prairie chicken **12**:726–727
prairie dog **5**:308; **12**:728–729
prairie rattlesnake **12**:763
prairies **7**:392
Prairie vole **16**:967
Prairie wolf *See* coyote
praying mantis **12**:730–731
Prehensile-tailed porcupine
    12:720–721
prickly pear **3**:139
prides **9**:528
primates **6**:330–331, 348–349;
    8:510–511
    See also ape(s); monkey(s)
proboscis **3**:135; **4**:222; **10**:595
Proboscis monkey **12**:732–733
prokaryotes **1**:56
pronghorn **1**:42–43
pronking **6**:352; **14**:862, 863
protoctists (protists) **1**:24–25, 30–31
protozoans **1**:30–31
Przewalski's horse **7**:440, 441
pseudopodia **1**:30, 31
ptarmigan **10**:599; **12**:734–735;
    15:945
pteridophytes (the fern group)
    5:306
Puff adder **15**:958, 959
puffer fish **12**:736–737

Volume numbers are in **boldface type** followed by colons.
Page numbers in **boldface type** indicate full articles.

puffin **12:738–739; 14:**841

puma (Mountain lion) **1:**41, 44; **12:**721, **740–741; 15:**907

pumpkin **14:**864

pupae/pupation

butterfly **3:**134–135, 135, 137

caddis fly **3:**141

crane fly **4:**223

firefly **5:**313

flea **5:**317

hawk moth **10:**595–596

silkworm **13:**838, 839

Purple (Common) foxglove **6:**336–337

Purple gallinule **6:**351

Purple granadilla **11:**679

Purple loosestrife **3:**157

Purple martin **15:**954–955

Purple pitcher plant **11:**702

Pussy willow **16:**1006, 1007

puya **2:**122, 123

Pygmy chimpanzee **3:**168, 169

Pygmy hippopotamus **7:**429

Pygmy marmoset **9:**558

pygmy mouse **10:**602

Pygmy nuthatch **10:**621

pygmy owl **11:**665, 666

Pygmy rattlesnake **8:**469; **12:**763

Pygmy shrew **13:**827

Pyrenean desman **10:**583

python(s) **1:**32, 33; **12:742–743,** 758

QR

quail **12:744–745**

quaking aspen **16:**1007

queen bees **2:**88

Queen-of-the-night **3:**138

Queensland (Australian) lungfish **9:**540, 541

quetzal **12:746–747**

quillwort **3:**179; **12:748–749**

quinidine **3:**175

quinine **3:**174–175; **4:**241

rabbit **7:**412; **12:750–751; 14:**883

rabies **2:**81; **6:**334, 335; **14:**842

raccoon **10:**608; **11:**673; **12:**741, **752–753; 14:**882, 883; **15:**955

radiolarians **1:**31

Raffia palm **11:**670

rafflesia **12:754–755**

ragweed **14:**888

Rainbowbird **2:**90

Rainbow trout **15:**940–941

Rainbow wrasse **16:**1017

rainforest **11:**648; **12:756–759**

temperate **12:**756; **15:**915

rat **10:**600–601; **12:760–761; 14:**883

Common (Brown) **10:**600–601; **12:**760, 761; **15:**954

cotton **4:**215

kangaroo **4:**248; **8:480–481; 10:**600; **13:**803

ratel (Honey badger) **1:**60, 61; **7:**432–433; **14:**863

Ratel's honeyguide **1:**61

rattlesnake **12:**729, **762–763; 13:**830–831; **15:**959; **16:**982

Pygmy **8:**469

raven **12:764–765; 13:**793

ray **12:766–767**

Red admiral butterfly **14:**875

red algae **1:**24

Red-and-green macaw **9:**544, 545

Red-billed hornbill **7:**434, 435

Red-billed oxpecker **11:**669

Red birch **2:**96

Red bird of paradise **2:**99

Red-breasted merganser **9:**564, 565

Red cardinal **14:**852

Red-crowned parrot **11:**676

Red deer **4:**243, 244; **5:**298

redds **13:**797; **15:**941

Red fox **4:**233; **6:**334–335; **15:**955

Red grouper **4:**211

Red grouse **7:**417

Red-headed weaver **16:**986, 987

Red honeysuckle **2:**71

Red kangaroo **8:**478, 479

Red land crab **4:**218, 219

Red (American) mangrove **9:**552–553; **16:**992

Red maple **9:**554, 555; **16:**992

Red-necked grebe **7:**394, 395

Red panda **11:**672, 673

Red (Natterer's) piranha **11:**700

Red Sea fan coral **4:**208

Red-shouldered hawk **7:**414, 415

Red-throated loon **9:**538, 539

red tides **1:**25

Red (Bald) uakari **15:**952, 953

Red-winged blackbird **2:**102, 103; **16:**991

Red wolf **16:**1010, 1011

Reef fish **16:**1016

Regent bowerbird **2:**119

reindeer (European caribou) **3:**151; **4:**243; **9:**521

reindeer lichen **9:**521

reptiles

with a shell **15:**924–925, 934–935, 948–951

and water-loss **4:**248

See also crocodilians; lizard(s); snake(s)

Resplendent quetzal **12:**746, 747

Reticulated python **12:**742, 743

rhea **13:774–775**

rhinoceros **13:776–779**

Rhinoceros beetle **2:**93

Rhinoceros hornbill **7:**434, 435

Rhipidistrian fish **3:**191

rhizoids **9:**533; **10:**592; **16:**1001

rhizomes **2:**100; **5:**306; **12:**719; **16:**1000

rhododendron **10:**598; **15:**914, 915

rice **13:780–781**

Ringed kingfisher **8:**488

Ringed seal **12:**714

Ringed storm petrel **11:**690

Ring-necked pheasant **11:**692, 693

Ring-tailed lemur **8:**510, 511

ringworm **6:**346; **12:**719

rivers **8:502–503; 16:**992

roadrunner **4:**231; **13:782–783**

robin **13:784–785; 15:**916

Robin moth **10:**597

Rock ape (Barbary ape; Barbary macaque) **2:72–73**

rock barnacle **15:**926

Rock cavy **7:**402, 403

Rock dove **5:**268, 269

rock hyrax **8:**458–459

Rock (Sugar) maple **9:**554, 555

rock rose **13:**802

rockweed **15:**926

rodents **2:**86–87; **3:**146–147, 170–171; **5:**266–267; **6:**332–333, 356–357; **7:**396–397, 402–403, 410–411, **8:**480–481, 508–509; **10:**600–603, 608–609, 622–623; **12:**712–713, 720–721, 728–729, 760–761; **14:**868–869; **16:**966–967

fleas on **5:**316

Roof (Black) rat **10:**600–601; **12:**760–761

rook **4:**229

roots **3:**138

aerial **9:**552, 553

buttress **12:**757

hair-like **4:**247

taproots **4:**239, 247; **6:**366

rose **13:786–787**

Rose-breasted cockatoo **3:**183

rose hips **13:**786–787

rosettes **1:**29

Rosy maidenhair fern **5:**307

Round-tailed muskrat **10:**608, 609

Royal albatross **1:**23

rubber tree **5:**310; **13:788–789**

Ruby-throated hummingbird **7:**446, 447

ruff **13:790–791**

Ruffed grouse **7:**400–401

Ruffed lemur **8:**511

Rufous-breasted hermit hummingbird **7:**446

Rufous elephant-shrew **5:**296, 297

Rufous hummingbird **7:**447

running pine **3:**178

Russian desman **10:**583

Russian dwarf hamster **7:**410

rust, coffee leaf **4:**199

Rusty blackbird **2:**102, 103

S

sable **15:**903

Sacred (Hamadryas) baboon **1:**54, 55

Volume numbers are in **boldface type** followed by colons.
Page numbers in **boldface type** indicate full articles.

acred ibis 8:462
age grouse 7:400, 401
go 4:237
go palm 4:236, 237
guaro cactus 3:138, 139
hara Desert 4:246, 247, 248
iga 13:792–793
lamander 1:52, 53; 13:794–795
  Cave (manfish) 3:158, 159
lmon 8:502; 13:796–797
ltwater (Estuarine) crocodile
  4:226
ltwater fish 1:34–37; 2:74–75;
  3:188–191; 6:326–327;
  7:398–399, 408–409, 426–427;
  9:530–531, 556–557;
  10:630–631; 11:698–699;
  12:736–737; 13:806–807;
  15:942–943; 16:1016–1017
maras 9:555
mbar 4:244; 13:798–799
moan flying fox 6:328
nara scorpion 13:801
nd fly 5:319
ndhill crane 4:220, 221
nd (Gould's) monitor 10:586,
  587
ndpiper 15:945
ndstorms 4:249
ndy shores 15:927
n Pedro fig 5:311
p 9:558
  aloe 1:28
  arum 1:46
  maple 9:555
  palm 11:671
  poppy 12:719
rgasso Sea 5:288, 289; 8:483
rgassum pipefish 11:699
tin bowerbird 2:118, 119
vannah baboon 1:54
vannas 7:392
wbill (Common merganser)
  9:564, 565
wfly, Larch 8:507
w grass 16:992
w-scaled viper 15:959
le bug 8:499
aled quail 12:744
ales

butterfly wing 3:137
  fish 3:153
  pangolin 11:674
Scaly-sided merganser 9:565
scaly tailed squirrel 6:333
Scaly-throated honeyguide 7:433
Scarlet ibis 8:462
Scarlet macaw 12:757
Scarlet passionflower 11:678, 679
scent glands 1:60; 8:459
Schaus swallowtail butterfly 3:134
Scimitar-horned oryx 11:656
scorpion 13:800–801
scorpion fish 4:211
Scotch heather 7:416, 417
Scots pine 11:694, 695; 12:716
Screwworm fly 5:319
scrubland 13:802–803
sea anemone 7:423; 13:804–805;
  15:927
seabirds 1:22–23; 6:338–339;
  7:404–405; 11:690–691;
  12:738–739; 14:840–841;
  15:922–923
Sea catfish 3:155
sea cow See dugong; manatee
sea cucumber 10:628, 629
sea grass 4:210; 9:548
sea horse 13:806–807
Sea Island cotton 4:215
seal 12:714, 717; 13:808–809;
  16:974, 975
Sea lamprey 8:504, 505
Sea lettuce 1:25; 8:483; 15:926
sea lion 13:809, 810–811; 16:974
sea mammals 5:262–263,
  276–277; 9:548–549;
  12:722–723; 13:808–811;
  16:974–975, 994–997
Sea otter 11:662–663; 13:813
sea slug (nudibranch) 14:871
sea star 15:927
Sea trout 15:941
sea turtle 15:950–951
sea urchin 13:812–813; 15:927
sea wasp 8:476

seaweed 1:24, 25; 8:482–483;
  10:626; 15:926
Secretary bird 13:814–815
Sedge warbler 4:230
seeds 2:120
  dispersal 4:239; 6:383; 12:719;
    14:879
  dormancy 4:247
  mustard 10:611
  poppy 12:719
  rice 13:781
  sesame 13:818–819
  soybean 14:850–851
  strawberry 14:879
  sunflower 14:889
  winged 9:555
self-pollination 6:380
Senegal acacia 1:17
Sensitive (Humble) plant
  9:568–569
sepals 9:546; 11:678
sepia 14:867
sequoia 13:816–817
sesame 13:818–819
Seven spot ladybug 8:499
shark 9:557; 13:820–823
  Great white 4:211; 13:820,
    821, 822
Sharp-shinned hawk 7:415
Sharp-tailed grouse 7:401
Sharptooth catfish 8:503
shearwater 14:840
sheep
  Barbary 6:368
  Bighorn 2:94–95; 10:599
shell
  for hermit crabs 7:422–423
  snail 14:849
  terrapin 15:924–925
  tortoise 15:934, 935
shields 4:204, 205
shoebill (Shoe-billed stork)
  13:824–825
shorelines 15:926–927
Short-nosed echidna 5:286, 287
Short-tailed albatross 1:23

Short-tailed leaf-nosed bat 2:78,
  79
Short-tailed monitor 10:586
Short-tailed weasel (ermine)
  16:984, 985
Shovelnose sturgeon 14:881
shrew 13:826–827
shrew mole 10:582
Shrew mouse 10:602
shrimp 13:828–829; 15:927
Siamang gibbon 6:359
Siberian chipmunk 3:171
Siberian tit 3:167
Side-striped jackal 8:472
sidewinder 12:792; 13:830–831
Sikkim larch 8:506
silk
  silkworm 14:838, 839
  spider 14:856–859
silkworm moth (Bombycidae)
  10:596; 14:838–839
  See also Giant silkworm moth
    (Saturniidae)
Silky anteater 1:40, 41
Silver-backed (Black-backed) jackal
  8:472
silverbacks 6:376–377
Silver fox 6:335
Silver maple 9:555
Simien jackal 8:472
single-celled organisms 1:30–31,
  56–59
Six-banded armadillo 1:44
skate 12:766
Skipjack tuna 15:942–943
skua 12:738; 14:840–841
skunk 1:60; 14:842–843
skunk cabbage 1:46, 47; 16:992
sleeping sickness 5:318; 9:553
Slippery Dick wrasse 16:1017
sloth 14:844–845
Sloth bear 2:82, 83, 85
slug 14:846–847
Smallmouth bass 2:76
Small-mouthed sea star (Blood star)
  14:870, 871
Small-scaled tree pangolin 11:675
Smyrna fig 5:311
snail 14:848–849
Snail kite 9:526

Volume numbers are in **boldface type** followed by colons.
Page numbers in **boldface type** indicate full articles.

snake(s) **1**:32–33; **3**:180–181; **12**:742–743, 762–763; **13**:830–831; **15**:958–959; **16**:982–983
  and roadrunners **13**:783
  and secretary birds **13**:814
snapping turtle **8**:503; **10**:608; **15**:948, 949, 950
snowdrop **9**:523
Snow goose **6**:372, 373, 374, 375
Snow gum **5**:302
Snow leopard **9**:519; **10**:599
Snowshoe hare **9**:542
Snowy owl **11**:666
Sociable weaver **16**:986, 987
social hornet **16**:978
social insects *See* ant; termite
Sockeye salmon **13**:796
soft-shelled turtle **15**:950
solitary wasp **16**:978
Somali wild donkey **5**:264
Sooty tern **15**:922
South American lungfish **9**:540–541
South American manatee **9**:549
South American (Brazilian) tapir **15**:906, 907
South American tree porcupine **12**:720–721
Southern anaconda **1**:32
Southern black widow spider **2**:106
Southern giant petrel **11**:690
Southern hairy-nosed wombat **16**:1012
Southern magnolia **9**:546, 547
Southern masked weaver **16**:987
Southern tamandua **1**:40, 41
soybean **14:850–851**
spadefoot toad **15**:931
spaghetti squash **14**:865
Spanish moss **2**:123; **9**:553
sparrow **14:852–853,** 883
  House **13**:785; **14**:852–853
Sparrow hawk **8**:484, 485; **14:854–855**
spatterdock **16**:980
spawn **10**:629
spawning
  salmon **13**:797
  trout **15**:940–941
  tuna **15**:943

Spectacled bear **2**:82, 85
Spectacled (Indian) cobra **3**:180, 181
sperm whale **14**:867; **16**:994, 995, 996
Sphagnum moss **16**:991
spider **14:856–859**; **16**:979
  bird-eating **15**:909
  Black widow **2:106–107; 14**:858
  jumping **10**:599; **14**:857, 858
spider crab **4**:218
spider plant **14:860–861**
spider wasp **16**:979
spike moss **3**:179
spine(s)
  echidna **5**:287
  hedgehog **7**:419
  leaf **3**:138
  porcupine **12**:720, 721
  sea urchin **13**:812
  tenrec **15**:919
Spiny anteater (Short-nosed echidna) **5**:286, 287
Spiny lobster **9**:537
spiracles **3**:134; **9**:567
Spitting cobra **3**:181
spitting spider **14**:857–858
Spix's (Little blue) macaw **9**:545
Splashing tetra **11**:701
sponge **15**:927
sporangia **3**:178–179
spores **6**:345; **9**:533; **12**:749; **16**:1001
sporophylls **3**:178
sporophytes **3**:179; **5**:306; **9**:533; **10**:592; **16**:1001
Spotted bowerbird **2**:118–119
Spotted hyena **8**:457
Spotted owl **11**:667
Spotted parsley (Poison hemlock) **7**:420–421
Spotted (White) piranha **11**:700
Spotted puffer fish **12**:736, 737
springbok **14:862–863**
Spring peeper **16**:992

spruce **10**:598; **15**:903, 915; **16**:991
Square-lipped rhinoceros **13**:776
squash **14:864–865**
squid **1**:22, 23; **14:866–867**
squirrel **14:868–869**; **16**:1015
  flying **6:332–333; 15**:903
  ground **4**:248; **12**:728
  scaly tailed **6**:333
  tree **14**:868–869
  See also chipmunk; prairie dog
Squirrel monkey **15**:953
Stag beetle **2**:93
Staghorn coral **4**:207
Stag's horn mos **3**:178
stamens **9**:546; **11**:678; **14**:875
staphylococcus **1**:58
starfish **14:870–871**
  Crown-of-thorns **4**:209, 211
starling **13**:785; **14:872–873**
Star-nosed mole **10**:582, 583
steamer duck **5**:274
Steelhead trout **15**:940, 941
Stellar's jay **15**:916–917
Steller's sea cow **9**:548
Steller's sea lion **13**:810, 811
stems **3**:138
  bamboo **1**:62, 63
  water-storage in **4**:247
steppes **7**:392
stickleback **8**:501
stigmas **11**:678
stinging nettle **14:874–875**
stingray **12**:767
stonefish **4**:211; **9**:531
stork **14:876–877**
  Marabou **14**:877; **16**:969
  Shoe-billed **13:824–825**
  Wood **14**:876–877; **16**:992, 993
storm petrel **11**:690–691
stotting **6**:352
Strangler fig **5**:310, 311
strawberry **13**:786; **14:878–879**
streptomyces bacteria **1**:59
Striped hyena **8**:457

Striped (Common) skunk **14**:842–843
strobili **3**:178, 179; **4**:237; **6**:363, 367; **16**:988
sturgeon **14:880–881**
styles **11**:678
suburban habitat **14:882–883**
succulents **1**:28; **3**:138
sugar **11**:671; **14**:884–885
sugar beet **14**:884
sugarcane **13**:780; **14:884–885**
Sugar maple **9**:554, 555; **15**:915
Sugar pine **11**:694
Sulfur-crested cockatoo **3**:182, 18
Sumatran rhinoceros **13**:778
Sumatran tiger **15**:928
summer squash **14**:865
Sun bear **2**:82, 85
sunbird **2**:100, 101; **14:886–887**
sundew **15**:957; **16**:991
sunfish **8**:503; **10**:630–631
sunflower **4**:239; **14:888–889**
sun pitcher **11**:702
surgeonfish **4**:208
Surinam toad **15**:931
swallow **4**:233; **14:890–891; 15**:954–955
swallowtail butterfly **3**:134, 137
Swamp cypress **13**:816
swamps **9**:527; **16**:992
Swamp wallaby **16**:972, 973
swan **14:892–893**
Sweet bay magnolia **9**:547
Sweet potato **12**:724
swift **14:894–895**
swim bladders **3**:188; **9**:540; **13**:806
swimmerets **9**:536; **13**:829
symbiosis **4**:208; **9**:520
Szechwan jumping mouse **10**:603

T
tadpoles **6**:343; **15**:930
tahr **6**:369
taiga **15:902–903**
Tailed frog **6**:343
Tailless (Common) tenrec **15**:918–919
tails **6**:341

Volume numbers are in **boldface type** followed by colons.
Page numbers in **boldface type** indicate full articles.

breaking off **7**:406
 prehensile **11**:647
marack **8**:507
marin **9**:558; **15:904–905**
nager **14**:852
nnin **1**:17; **7**:421; **9**:552; **13**:817
pir **15:906–907**
proots **4**:239, 247; **6**:366
rantula **15:908–909**
rantula-hawk wasp **16**:978
rpan **7**:441
asmanian devil **15:910–911**
awny owl **11**:666
a **15:912–913**
ak **12**:759
eth
 aardvark **1**:15
 hare and rabbit **12**:750
 See also canines; incisors; molars
emmincks ground (Cape)
 pangolin **11**:675
mperate forest **12**:756;
 15:914–917
mperature, body **10**:586; **11**:687;
 13:783; **14**:845
ndrils **6**:380; **11**:678, 679, 703
nrec **15:918–919**
ntacles
 hydra **8**:454, 455
 polyp **4**:207
 sea anemone **13**:804, 805
 snail **14**:848
 squid **14**:866
rmite **1**:14, 15; **9**:562; **10**:619;
 11:674–675; **15:920–921**
n **14**:840; **15:922–923; 16**:991
rapin **15:924–925**
 Diamond-back **15**:924–925;
  16:991
 European pond **8**:502
tudines *See* terrapin; tortoise;
 turtle
ra **11**:701
xas horned lizard **8**:465
llus **9**:533
ick-tailed (Greater) galago **6**:349
stle finch **6**:371
omson's gazelle **6**:352, 353
orn apple **4**:241
orns **1**:17; **13**:787

thorn tree *See* acacia
Thread fin butterfly fish **7**:398–399
Thread herring **7**:427
thread-like bacteria **1**:59
Three-toed anteater **1**:40
three-toed sloth **14**:844
Thrush nightingale **10**:613
tick **15:906–907**
tide pool and coast **15:926–927**
tides **15**:926
tiger **15**:907, **928–929**
tiger lily **14**:860
Tiger salamander **1**:52, 53
tiger shrimp **13**:828
Timber wolf **16**:1010
toad **6**:343–344; **15:930–931**
toadfish **12**:736
toadlets **15**:931
toadstool **6**:347
Tobacco hawk moth **4**:233;
 10:594–596
tobacco plant **4**:241
Toco toucan **15**:936, 937
Toddy palm **11**:671
Tokay gecko **6**:354
tomato **4**:241; **12**:724; **15:932–933**
tools **11**:649, 662–663
tortoise **15:934–935**
tortoiseshell **15**:951
toucan **15:936–937**
toucanet **15**:936, 937
trapdoor spider **14**:857
Traveler's palm **2**:101
Tree cricket **4**:225
tree frog **6**:341, 343; **11**:703
tree kangaroo **15:938–939**
tree line **10**:598
trees
 broad-leaved **2**:96
 tundra **15**:945
 See also forests
Tree snail **14**:848
tree squirrel **14**:868–869
troglodytes (cavernicoles)
 3:158–159
trogons **12**:746–747

troops, monkey **1**:54, 55; **4**:201;
 9:550–551; **12**:732
Tropical rat flea **5**:317
trout **15:940–941**
true bacteria **1**:58–59
Trumpeter swan **14**:892
trunkfish (sunfish) **10**:630–631
trunks, elephant **5**:292, 293
tsetse fly **5**:318; **9**:553
tubers **12**:725
Tufted puffin **12**:738
tulip **9**:523; **14**:860
tuna **15:942–943**
 Bluefin **10**:629; **15**:942, 943
tundra **4**:249; **10**:606; **15:944–945**
Tundra swan **14**:892
tunny (Bluefin tuna) **10**:629;
 15:942, 943
turkey **15:946–947**
Turkey buzzard (Turkey vulture)
 16:968, 969
Turkey vulture **16**:968, 969
Turk's cap lily **9**:522
turtle **15:948–951**
 snapping **8**:503; **10**:608;
  15:948, 949, 950
Turtle dove **5**:269
tusks
 elephant **5**:293, 294
 narwhal **16**:994
 walrus **16**:974
 warthog **16**:976, 977
two-toed sloth **14**:844

UV
uakari **15:952–953**
Umbrella pine **13**:816
Umbrella tree **9**:547
ungulates
 odd-toed **15**:906
 See also hoofed mammals
Upside-down jellyfish **8**:476, 477
urban habitat **15:954–955**
Utah prairie dog **12**:729
vanilla plant **11**:650, 651
vascular plants **12**:748

velvet, antler **4**:243, 244
venison **13**:799
venom
 fish **9**:530
 Gila monster **6**:361
 puffer fish **12**:737
 scorpion **13**:801
 snake **3**:180–181; **12**:762;
  15:958, 959; **16**:983
 spider **14**:858; **15**:909
 See also poison
Venus flytrap **15:956–957; 16**:991
Victoria, Lake **8**:500
vicuna **3**:145; **9**:534, 535
viper **12**:792; **15:958–959; 16**:983
 McMahon's **13**:831
Virginia (Common) opossum
 11:646–647; **15**:955
vole **16:966–967**
vulture **16:968–969**

W
wading birds **1**:50–51; **4**:204–205,
 220–221, 234–235; **5**:314–315;
 6:350–351; **7**:424–425;
 8:462–463, 470–471, 486–487;
 9:526–527; **13**:790–791,
 824–825; **14**:876–877
Walking fern **5**:307
walking stick **16:970–971**
wallaby **16:972–973**
walrus **16:974–975**
Wandering albatross **1**:22, 23
wapiti (elk) **4**:244; **5:298–299**
warbler **16**:992
 Sedge **4**:230
warthog **16:976–977**
wasp **16:978–979**
 Fig **5**:311
waterbirds **11**:684–685
water boatman **3**:172
waterfowl **5**:272–275; **6**:372–375;
 7:394–395; **9**:564–565;
 14:892–893
Water hemlock **7**:421
water lily **16:980–981**
Water moccasin **10**:608;
 16:982–983, 993
water mouse **10**:600, 601–602
Water opossum **11**:646

Volume numbers are in **boldface type** followed by colons.
Page numbers in **boldface type** indicate full articles.

water rat, Florida (Round-tailed muskrat) **10**:608, 609

water shrew **13**:826

water table **16**:990–991

Waterwheel plant **15**:957

weasel **5**:307–308; **13**:827; **16**:984–985

weasel family **1**:60–61; **9**:570–571; **11**:662–663, 696–697; **14**:842–843; **16**:984–985

weaver **16**:986–987

Wedge-tailed eagle **5**:279

Weedy seadragon **13**:806

Weeping willow **16**:1006, 1007

weevil **2**:92

welwitschia **16**:988–989

West African live-bearing toad **15**:931

West Australian dwarf python **12**:742

Western bluebird **2**:110

Western diamondback rattlesnake **12**:762, 763

Western European hedgehog **7**:418, 419

Western larch **8**:506, 507

Western lowland gorilla **6**:376

Western white pine **11**:695

West Indian (North American) manatee **9**:548, 549

wetlands **9**:527; **12**:749; **16**:990–993

cattail marshes **3**:157

whale **13**:829; **16**:994–997

Blue **10**:628–629; **13**:816; **16**:994, 995, 996, 997

Humpback **16**:994, 995–996

Killer **5**:263; **11**:687; **16**:996, 997

sperm **14**:867; **16**:994, 995, 996

White (beluga) **14**:881; **16**:995, 996

Whale-headed stork (shoebill) **13**:824–825

Whale shark **13**:821, 823

wheat **4**:232; **16**:998–999

whirling whips (dinoflagellates) **1**:25

whisk fern **16**:1000–1001

Whistling swan **14**:892, 893

White-breasted nuthatch **10**:620, 621

White cedar **16**:992

White-collared swift **14**:895

White-faced ibis **8**:462

White-footed mouse **10**:601, 602–603; **12**:731

white-footed (deer) mouse **10**:600, 602–603

White-handed gibbon **6**:358

White ibis **8**:462, 463

White-lipped peccary **11**:683

White marlin **9**:557

White mustard **10**:610–611

White (Spotted) piranha **11**:700

White rat **12**:761

White rhinoceros **13**:776–777, 778, 779

White-spotted gecko **6**:355

White stork **14**:876

White-tailed deer **4**:242, 244, 245

White-tailed fish eagle **12**:739

White tern **15**:923

White (Bald) uakari **15**:952, 953

White water lily **16**:980

White whale (beluga) **14**:881; **16**:995, 996

Whooping crane **4**:220, 221

Wild boar **15**:917

Wild cat **16**:1002–1003

wild dog, African **1**:20–21; **4**:255; **16**:1005

wildebeest **16**:1004–1005, 1023

Wild passionflower **11**:679

wild rice **13**:780

Wild turkey **15**:946, 946–947, 947

willow **15**:945; **16**:1006–1007

Willow ptarmigan (Willow grouse) **12**:734, 735; **15**:945

Wilson's storm petrel **11**:690, 691

Windmill palm **11**:670

wind pollination **2**:97; **4**:213; **6**:383; **14**:875; **16**:998

wine **6**:381; **11**:671

winged insects *See* insects, winged

wings

of bats **2**:78–79

broken **5**:274

butterfly **3**:135, 137

spurs on **8**:470

winter squash **14**:865

wisent (European bison) **1**:18–19; **2**:125

wobbegong **13**:821, 822

wolf **4**:255; **10**:606–607; **13**:792; **15**:903, 917, 945; **16**:1008–1011

Prairie or Brush wolf (coyote) **4**:216–217

wolverine **15**:945

wombat **15**:910; **16**:1012–1013

wood (timber)

eucalypt **5**:302

larch **8**:507

maple **9**:555

oak **10**:624

palm **11**:671

pine **11**:695

wood anemone **15**:916

Wood buffalo **2**:125

woodchuck (groundhog) **7**:396–397

Wood duck **14**:873

Wood ibis **14**:876–877; **16**:992, 993

Woodland jumping mouse **10**:603

woodlouse **9**:566

wood partridge (quail) **12**:744–745

woodpecker **15**:917; **16**:1014–1015

woodpecker family **7**:432–433; **16**:1014–1015

Wood pigeon **5**:269; **14**:854

wood rat **12**:761

Wood stork **14**:876–877; **16**:992, 993

woody plants with cones **4**:236–237; **6**:366–367; **8**:506–507; **11**:694–695; **13**:816–817; **16**:988–989

Woolly (Austrian) foxglove **6**:337

woolly opossum **11**:646

woolly rhinoceros **13**:776

worm casts **5**:283

worm(s) **5**:282–283

wrasse **16**:1016–1017

Cleaner **4**:211; **7**:399; **16**:1016 1017

wren, Flightless **8**:469

XYZ

xerophytes **2**:71; **4**:246; **6**:367

yak **16**:1018–1019

yeast **6**:344, 346

Yellow baboon **1**:54

Yellow bark **3**:175

Yellow-bellied sapsucker **16**:1015

Yellow-bellied sunbird **14**:886

Yellow-billed loon **9**:538

Yellow-billed oxpecker **11**:668, 669

Yellow birch **2**:96, 97

Yellow-browed toucanet **15**:937

yellow fever **10**:590

Yellowfin tuna **15**:943

Yellow granadilla **11**:679

Yellow-headed blackbird **2**:102

Yellow perch **11**:688, 689

Yellow skunk cabbage **1**:47

Yellow stingray **12**:767

Yellow water lily **16**:980

Yerba maté **7**:431

yucca **16**:1020–1021

zebra **1**:21; **7**:392; **16**:1022–1023

Zebra fish *See* lionfish

Zigzag heron **7**:424

zoos, and pandas **11**:673

zoospores **6**:345

zucchini **14**:864, 865

Volume numbers are in **boldface type** followed by colons.
Page numbers in **boldface type** indicate full articles.